FOOTBALL AND GANGSTERS

Graham Johnson is a full-time crime writer and author of the bestselling *Powder Wars* and *Druglord*. He is a former investigations editor at the *Sunday Mirror* and during ten years on Fleet Street covered subjects including child slavery, people smuggling, drugs and the Balkan Wars.

FOOTBALL AND GANGSTERS

HOW ORGANISED CRIME CONTROLS THE BEAUTIFUL GAME

GRAHAM JOHNSON

MAINSTREAM PUBLISHING

EDINBURGH AND LONDON

This edition, 2007

Copyright © Graham Johnson, 2006
All rights reserved
The moral right of the author has been asserted

First published in Great Britain in 2006 by
MAINSTREAM PUBLISHING COMPANY (EDINBURGH) LTD
7 Albany Street
Edinburgh EH1 3UG

ISBN 9781845962470

The author and publishers wish to thank *The Independent* newspaper for
allowing extracts from an interview with footballer Mark Ward to be used in
this book. The original article, headlined 'Mark Ward: From No. 7 to
Prisoner Number NM6982', carried an exclusive interview with Ward by
Independent journalist Nick Harris and appeared on 16 November 2005

A catalogue record for this book is available from the British Library

Typeset in Frutiger and Garamond

Printed in Great Britain by
Cox and Wyman Ltd, Reading

Contents

Introduction

Soccer and Crime: the Culture

Football and Gangsters is an exposé of organised crime in football today. Britain's top gangsters have a lot more pull on and off the pitch than is healthy – and a lot more than the terrified sporting authorities would care to admit. It's not surprising that one of Britain's wealthiest sectors – crime – would want to invest some of its hard-earned cash, or use some of its extraordinary power, to get a foothold in another of the country's leading money-spinners: football. However, what is shocking is that little has been done to curb the sinister influences. Football and gangsters is still an unspeakable taboo.

This book reveals how young players in the Premiership are especially vulnerable to gangsters because of their glamorous lifestyles, popularised on TV in programmes such as ITV's *Footballers' Wives* and Sky's *Dream Team*. Gangsters often use sophisticated methods of entrapment, including drugs, prostitutes and 'honeytraps', to blackmail players, who are often too young, too scared or too stupid to be wary in the first place or to report incidents of extortion to the police afterwards. The culture of 'roasting' female admirers, binge drinking and general out-of-control cockiness amongst young players today has given the underworld ample ammunition to penetrate the heart of football, and it's no accident that many of these lurid stories end up in the papers. They are often planted there by manipulative underworld godfathers to get control of the players where it hurts. One of Britain's most well-known villains admitted, 'If you've got dirt on a player, you've got him by the bollocks. And if you've got a ten- or twenty-million-pound player by the bollocks, then you've got the club by the bollocks as well. These players are the club's main assets. It's not a sophisticated way of getting control – and that's what it's all about – but it works. Control opens a lot of opportunities to people like me.'

A former security consultant for a Premiership team revealed that clubs in general were not yet doing enough to protect their players adequately from the grip of crime. He said that the vast majority of clubs were not even prepared to admit there was a problem. However, the security consultant did concede that a very small number of top clubs had implemented some rudimentary measures to safeguard their players' exposure to blackmailers and so on. These were mainly preventative, including background checks to look for vices before signing players and using private detectives to follow their every move in the run-up to a proposed transfer to find out if their lifestyles were scandal-free. In that way, the wealthy teams hoped they could make a fair assessment of a player's susceptibility to penetration by organised crime before they were allowed into their hallowed club.

The consultant, who refused to be identified after receiving threats himself, added: 'On the whole, most clubs have no risk-assessment strategies concerning organised crime. That's like taking your gate receipts on a Saturday afternoon and leaving them in the street. One or two of the big clubs have recently begun allocating resources to their security departments to protect themselves. For instance, one of the biggest clubs in the Premier League has taken to monitoring players and officials not only before they're signed but once they are actually working at the club. It's common sense, but it's surprising how much that kind of thing is overlooked. They secretly videotape even the most routine meetings at their facilities to find out if there are any criminal influences taking place. They use exactly the same private detectives who plant hidden videos to catch out ASBO kids smashing up phone boxes on housing estates. That's how scared they are of this type of thing getting a hold. The old mentality used to be once a player had made the grade and was in, he was in, and that's that. He was now a "club man" and could be relied upon to behave like the standards dictate. Now that approach is not good enough.'

A football agent with 20 years' experience and 30 players on his books added: 'The bottom line is this: what sponsor wants to read about their boy taking cocaine? The players know it's over when they get caught taking drugs or in a scandal, so that's why they would rather pay a villain ten or twenty grand to make it go away rather than inform me or the club that they've made a mistake. Half the problem is players keep it from us, so we just have this problem of the underworld influence creeping up into the clubs, but we don't know it's there. It's invisible. They've got us; they've got the chairmen – the lot – but we don't know it.'

The growth of gangsterism in the game began in the '60s, when East End villains tried to muscle in on clubs because of their money-washing potential. According to '60s Arsenal legend Peter Marinello: 'There were some dodgy characters and gangsters. The Richardson brothers were in the players' lounge at Highbury one time, until the manager, Bertie Mee, found out about it. I met one character at a party who asked me in all seriousness if I wanted him to shoot a rival teammate so I could get back in the side! Obviously, I recoiled in horror at the very thought, and the guy reassured me that "shoot" didn't mean murder – just a leg job. I almost said, "That's all right, then," but thought better of it.'

However, the jokey innocence of those days is long gone, mainly because of the vast amount of money in the modern game. The Premier League is now the richest league in the world, generating a staggering £1.25 billion annually – light years ahead of its closest rival, Italy's Serie A, with £800 million. The gates in the top division are the highest since the early 1950s, and the attendance figures for the entire League are the highest since 1964. Since the birth of the Premier League, an astronomical amount of TV money has flooded into football, not counting the obscene amount of cash from sponsorships and spin-offs. Today, street kids from Sri Lanka to São Paulo who do not have a pair of shoes to their name can list the squads rote-fashion of Liverpool, Man United, Chelsea and Arsenal simply because they can watch them regularly live on communal tellies. For the underworld, that means only one thing – ching! When villains threatened to shoot the foot of England and Liverpool hero Steven Gerrard to prevent him moving to Chelsea, the motives were a lot more complicated than they had been in Marinello's swinging '60s London.

There is also a long history of gangsters mixing with footballers, based on a mutual fascination that often leads to problems. It often starts early on, because many footballers are from working-class or even underclass backgrounds, often raised in rough areas where they rub shoulders with rising stars of the underworld from a young age. When they become rich and famous, footballers find it hard to cut their ties and are often dragged back into the gutter by their old mates. Drugs, drink, women, nightclubs, gambling – the traditional vices of the criminal world – become freely available to players when they hit the big-time and are hard to refuse.

As well as the lifestyle links, there are also the indefinable attractions, such as the magnetic appeal of success and simply that gangsters like to hang around with footballers in the way that rock stars do, or the way the Kray twins did with celebrities and vice versa in '60s London. It just happens. *Football and Gangsters* reveals a long list of soccer stars who have found it difficult to cut ties with their past and all the baggage that goes with it – and have eventually paid the price.

In 2005, Gary Lineker's agent, Jon Holmes, pointed out that it was the part played by mobsters in the Black Sox World Series baseball scandal that stimulated American authorities to impose stringent regulations on their national game. He called for the footballing authorities to clean up our own game. But the villains who are now firmly established in Britain's national sport are unlikely to be retrenched by the arrival of blazer-wearing officials from Soho Square. A leading gangster, who owns a football business, said, 'Once it starts, it's hard to stop. I'll give you an example. There's a fella who made millions with a rich underworld boss. He now owns a football club, which he still uses to clean his money. He's still at it today. The point is, he is very ambitious. He will just keep trading up until he's able to buy Man United, Chelsea or whoever, and though everyone knows he's a gangster, no one can do anything about it.'

A top policeman was equally pessimistic: 'Boxing used to be the sport of villains. They used it to network. A lot of deals used to get done at the boxing. Now it's football. That's the platform now, as boxing is dead.'

1

Wayne Rooney: the Gangsters Move In

In the summer of 2004, gangsters waged a terrifying campaign of death threats and violence against me after I launched a newspaper investigation into England wonderkid Wayne Rooney. Three different gun-toting gangs threatened to bash me up if I didn't go along with their variously shady programmes. Another underworld figure warned that I would be kidnapped, put in the boot of a car and taken to an 'abode' of his choice where I would be tied up and tortured if I didn't drop what I was doing. Another hot-tempered villain, the pimp-cum-boyfriend of a backstreet hooker, vowed to chop me up with a machete following the publication of a story which he claimed humiliated him. A crime godfather overlooking this unfolding drama predicted that my presence in Rooney's home town of Liverpool was threatening to plunge the city's notorious underworld elite into civil war, sparking a certain bloodbath amongst its rival factions. That's how much of a problem this was causing. What had I done wrong?

My only crime: to look into a story about a teenage football player with a penchant for £45-a-time prostitutes. Ten years ago, this type of 'footballer shagging story', as they are known in the trade, was relatively straightforward. Now it was safer to be a war reporter. I knew because I had been one.

FOOTBALL AND GANGSTERS

I had always heard of the links between football and gangsters, but now I was finding out first-hand that the underworld today had *direct* control of certain key elements of the beautiful game. And what's more, they were willing to police and increase their stake in Britain's most popular sport with the age-old tools of their trade: guns, knives and baseball bats.

The key question I kept asking myself was 'Why are some of the most dangerous gangsters in the British underworld getting so upset about a tabloid journalist going about his job of catching football players with their pants down?' It was nothing new; Fleet Street reporters had been doing it for years. What had changed to turn it into a big deal? That was what puzzled me. I told myself that there must have been a hidden agenda which I had overlooked. And it didn't take me long to work it out. It all came down to money – millions of pounds of it.

This first brush with football's secret underworld came in July 2004. I got a call from a very worried soccer insider saying that a gang of professional blackmailers were plotting to sting Wayne Rooney, who was seeing out his final months at Everton, for a few hundred grand. This came at a very messy time for Rooney. His business affairs were already getting very complicated. At the same time, he was at the centre of a completely separate alleged £1-million dispute between his old and his current football agents.

Paul Stretford was his current agent, and he did not agree that Peter McIntosh, the local players' representative who had first discovered the boy wonder, and his backer, John Hyland, had any remaining rights to the wonderkid's earnings. Hyland and McIntosh argued, quite understandably, that because they had discovered the footballing genius they were entitled to a piece of the action. Stretford tried to blag the pair off and, after a frustrating round of negotiations, relations became strained on both sides. Stretford then claimed things got violent. Hyland insisted that he wanted to settle the matter in a businesslike fashion.

Eventually, Cheshire Police investigated the allegations. McIntosh was not in the frame, but Hyland and two other business associates were charged with blackmail. The case went to court. Stretford was accused of lying under oath, and Hyland's camp were proved not guilty. The court case was viewed as a great victory for Hyland. The FA launched an investigation into Stretford's affairs, and Hyland and McIntosh are pursuing a £10-million civil case against him.

Rooney was left bewildered as he looked on at the messy and unsavoury circus of greed that had unfolded around him. His pure and magical success was seemingly being tainted before it had fully flowered. But he was determined to remain focused on his game, and it's a testimony to his character that he did not allow his football to be affected. The case will be dealt with later in the book.

However, the footballing star did not escape the wranglings completely unscathed, and an unpleasant surprise arose as an indirect consequence of the contractual dispute. While the police were busy chasing the innocent former agents through the courts, a gang of proper blackmailers were plotting to take advantage of the confusion by stinging Roo for real. Like many blackmailers before them, they were planning to use sex as the pretext for shaming the young star – who was going out with his high-profile fiancée Coleen McLoughlin – into coughing up dough. The gang had got wind of a seedy rumour that, if true, could help them achieve their pay day. They had heard that Roo had once paid for sex with a high-class escort girl. The twist in the tale was that the hooker was a twin – a unique selling point in the escort market. The sisters often visited clients together and could charge a premium for the service.

Professional blackmailers are as good, if not better, at gathering information as investigative journalists or even spies. The main advantage they have over people like me is that they are not constrained by rules or regulations, such as the Press Complaints Commission guidelines or criminal laws. Blackmailers often use dodgy private detectives to track down individuals by illegally extracting information from databases. Another arm of the extortion gang is employed to do surveillance, another to exploit witnesses using bribery and coercion and another as a rummage team to burgle houses, steal files and sift through rubbish to glean compromising information, known in the trade as 'bin spinning'.

During a successful intelligence-gathering phase, the blackmailers had discovered that the high-class escort girl who had allegedly had sex with Rooney had documentary evidence of the liaison in the form of a note that Rooney had written to her. For a criminal gang, this was a mouth-watering touch, because they could use it in a sting on Rooney by sending a copy to him to prove they had him by the balls. Faced with hard evidence, Rooney would find it hard to dismiss the blackmailers as chancers. A lot of famous people, and, in particular, footballers, attract a lot of chancers who routinely try to screw money out of them by simply pretending to have dirt on them, often having no evidence to back up the compromising claims they make in order to blackmail targets. The chancers – as opposed to serious blackmailers – try it on in the hope that celebs will pay them off just to remove the hassle. This phenomenon will also be dealt with later in the book. Anyway, armed with the note, the blackmailers were sure that Rooney and his camp would take them extremely seriously.

Despite the enormous amount of underworld activity going on around them, the prostitute and her sister had no idea that they were going to be used in this way. They were unwitting pawns in the game. The blackmailers were planning to get them to cooperate using coercion, intimidation and violence and force them to side with them against Rooney in a bid to make him pay over money. Usually, they would start off by telling the hookers that they would inform their families of their true occupation. Most young prostitutes are too ashamed to tell their parents what they do, for obvious reasons, especially if they live at home in a normal suburban house with mum and dad, as in this case.

However, eleventh-hour help was at hand – in the form of my good self. Luckily, my contact – the football professional who had tipped me off – had found out about the dastardly scheme before it was too late. The whistle-blower was a middle-ranking football executive who had worked in football for 20 years. He was genuinely horrified that two young girls and England's World Cup hope were going to be terrorised by ruthless men, and he'd decided to contact me. The streetwise football exec would not reveal the names of the gang members for fear of his own life, but he had come up with a counter-plan. He suggested that if I could get to the girls first, buy them up for a legitimate kiss-and-tell story and publicise the affair far and wide, it would spike the blackmailers' gun and mean an end to their intentions. It would take the sting out of their plan immediately. Too bad on Roo; he would have to suffer public embarrassment. The hookers would probably get a hard time as well. But, at the end of the day, it would save him and the prostitutes from coming to serious harm. It was the lesser of two evils, in his book. And that was that.

I was not totally convinced by my tipster's motives. Sources invariably have their own reasons for dishing out information, and these are seldom based on morality. However, it was not my job to worry about the meanings behind the facts he was giving me. My motives were purely journalistic. This was a great story, end of story. And if the facts were accurate, that was that as well.

He gave me several useful pieces of information, but my tipster did not give away any more details, even though he knew the name of the prostitutes and the agency they worked for. That would be down to me. Luckily, I had some very good contacts on the ground in Liverpool, and fortunately I was able to get a meeting in a pub with another football insider, a very knowledgeable professional, who also knew about Rooney's trysts with hookers. The Premiership is a hothouse of gossip, even worse than TV's *Footballers' Wives*. Secrets like this are often well known among a trusted few. Within hours, he was able to give me the first names of the hookers, the agency who employed them and some other crucial details. That's all I needed.

The agency was called La Femme. The prostitute who went with Wayne was called Charlotte Glover. And the next stage was for me to turn them over, as it's known in the trade. I booked a suite at the Marriott Hotel near Speke's John Lennon Airport. I chose the hotel specifically because it was a new hotel outside the city centre and therefore relatively gangster-free – I was well known to many of the 'community leaders' in Liverpool as I had been chasing many of them for years, and the last thing I needed was to be recognised in the course of such a sensitive story, for them to blow my cover and to ruin the investigation. My first task was to put in a blag call to the agency posing as a punter who had once booked the twins. I knew from my experience of doing loads of these stories that they wouldn't query a call out of the blue because every John looks and sounds the same to them. They'd just see it as repeat business. Unfortunately, the receptionist told me that the twins had recently left the firm to concentrate on their college work, so she couldn't offer me their services. In one way, that was good – she had confirmed the existence of the twins. But it was also bad – they were no longer doing the business, so there would be little chance of standing the story up. I sounded really disappointed, making it known that I'd be prepared to pay top dollar for the twins to do a star turn at a record-industry party.

I often posed as a music-industry executive, because it was a glamorous, socially mobile job which was flexible enough to be used as a front for lots of different investigations. I had a strong Liverpool accent because of my upbringing, and it was common for folk like myself to be running around in the 'anything goes' pop industry with lots of cash to spend on cocaine, prostitutes, celebrities and whatever else was going. It was the perfect cover for delving into many of the things that tabloid newspapers are interested in.

The receptionist told me that she would try to dig out a number for the twins and see if they wanted to come out of retirement for a bonus pay day. A short while later, I got a call from 21-year-old Charlotte Glover, the prostitute who'd had sex with Wayne Rooney, though she didn't tell me this until later.

I made an appointment to see her and her sister the following night. I got a load of champagne in – though not too much, as it is bad form to get witnesses drunk before extracting info from them – to make it look like a party. When they arrived, we had a drink and a chat. It was too risky to reveal who I was straight off or ask about Rooney, so I used a few old Fleet Street tricks to get everyone in the mood, so that I could extract the info subtly.

I started to boast about all of the celebs and pop stars I'd met in my fictitious job as a music-industry executive and all the mad stuff I'd got up to – all rubbish, of course, but designed to get the hookers onto the subject of famous people. At the end of the blag story, I quietly asked the girls whether they had ever met anyone famous in the line of their job and so on. 'Wayne Rooney,' said Charlotte straight off the bat. 'He booked me last year.' It was as simple as that. Game over. End of story. She came right out with it, straight to the point. 'He was a nobhead,' she added. 'He was just like this little scally. I didn't even know it was him.'

I pretended not to know who Wayne Rooney was, so as to seem a bit blasé about it and not give the game away. Both girls giggled and said how they had gone to see him and three of his mates at a pokey council house in Croxteth about a year before and that Charlotte had had sex with him in the bathroom.

By the way, I had hidden two secret video recorders and two minidisc digital tape recorders at various positions around the room to catch the evidence on tape.

Now that I had confirmation that the story was true from the main witness, I had to manipulate the situation so that the girls would be happy to do a kiss-and-tell story for the *Sunday Mirror*. This was easier said than done. I couldn't just ask them directly, because I'd have to reveal my real identity and my initial deception would make them angry and put them offside. It would have to be done subtly. Enter Investigator Two. *Sunday Mirror* snapper John Gladwin had been waiting in the lobby of the hotel all night trying to get sly pictures of the girls. I pretended to go to the toilet and phoned him on the mobile at about 1.30 a.m. I had asked John to pose as a bohemian, celeb-type PR man, and this was his cue. Minutes later, he wandered into the room in perfect character.

FOOTBALL AND GANGSTERS

It's the details that matter in a blag like this, and some of them were so funny that, on several occasions, I simply could not stop myself from laughing out loud. More than once, I had to cover up my giggles by blaming the champers, which had started to flow a bit by then. As soon as he entered the room, John camply removed his soft-skin shoes and sat cross-legged on the chair in an over-the-top impression of a flighty, boho, yoga-worshipping PR luvvie. At various points in the conversation, he also mimicked the habits of a cocaine-snorting showbiz whore, routinely wiping his nose and pretending to be over-alert, jumpy and a bit mad, something like a cross between *Absolutely Fabulous* and a drag-queen cabaret act. After a couple of glasses of champagne, I asked the girls to tell the PR man about their liaison with this young footballer. They repeated the story, having a bit of a laugh along the way. John responded by saying that he knew people in the newspapers who would pay good money for a story like that.

This is when the 'switch' occurred, to use a term favoured by con men everywhere. From this point on, once we had the girls' trust, the illusion of the party we were meant to be having, and the girls' supposed role in it, disappeared. Two hours later, we were sat in a hotel near Lytham St Annes, the *Sunday Mirror* were on the way, and the rest is Fleet Street history – or fish-and-chip paper, depending on which way you look at it.

The girls gave us a long and in-depth exposé, which I later worked up into a front-page story for the *Sunday Mirror*, along with four inside pages of further detail. It was published on 25 July 2004 and was a major Fleet Street scoop. One of the most astonishing and amusing aspects of the kiss and tell was a small note which Rooney had written to Charlotte after he had sex with her. The scribbled piece of paper was part laddish prank/part autograph/part boast by Rooney but, as far as the story was concerned, it was a mini signed confession which he could hardly deny – especially after I got it analysed by two of Britain's top handwriting experts and it came back as a positive match. The note stated: 'To Charlotte, I shagged u on 28 Dec. Loads of Love. Wayne Rooney.' Poetry.

At that point, Rooney had been engaged to Coleen McLoughlin for six months, having known her since the age of 12. Earlier that month, he sold a story to a newspaper for about £270,000 describing how he gave Coleen a 'fantastic' first night of passion in a hotel on Valentine's night. In the rose-tinted account of his love life, Rooney had also described how they had their first kiss behind a local church and bragged that Coleen was shocked at what a great kisser he was.

This information was fresh in the mind of Charlotte when I interviewed her, and she wasn't backwards in coming forward to voice her opinion about Rooney's behaviour. Almost immediately, she said, 'I couldn't believe he was paying me for sex at the same time as putting on this lovey-dovey act for Coleen. He's so two-faced.'

She went on to reveal how her seedy encounter happened three days after Christmas, on 28 December 2002. Rooney was only 17 and had just finished a game for Everton against Bolton at Goodison Park. The tryst ended with Charlotte having sex with Rooney on a grotty bathroom floor in a council house on a near-derelict estate. Charlotte took up the story: 'That night, the agency I worked for, La Femme, got a call for three girls to go to a flat in the Croxteth area of Liverpool. We got to there about 1.45 a.m. It was a depressing place, and we were scared because most of the other flats around it were boarded up and vandalised.

'Three of us – myself, my sister Katie and another escort girl – walked in and there were four men inside. The man who had phoned up opened the door. His name was Mark and I recognised him from the Jolly Miller pub where I worked part-time as a barmaid. There was also a baldy lad and a fair-haired guy.

'Then I noticed the lad sitting quietly in the corner with a Santa hat pulled over his head as though he didn't want us to recognise him. It was one of those orange hats with a bobble on the end and the letters WKD written on the side. They were giving them away free with bottles of WKD [an alcopop drink].

'My sister recognised him straight away and blurted out, "I'm sure that's Wayne Rooney," because she'd seen his picture in the local paper the day before.

'So I walked over and said, "Are you Wayne Rooney?"'

'I was really excited, because even though I'd been an escort for over a year by then I'd never been with someone famous. But he just said, "No, I'm a boxer," and turned away.

'But there was no mistaking it was Wayne Rooney, because he was dead ugly. He was wearing black trousers and a white Marks & Spencer shirt, and I started to flirt to make sure that I'd pair off with him.

'Rooney said that he would pay for himself and two of his mates to have sex with me, my sister and the other girl. Like always, before we did anything, I asked for the money up front. I didn't care who he was; he had to pay.

'It was £140 each, but they didn't have enough on them so Rooney gave the fair-haired lad his bank card and he left to go for some more cash. I remember laughing to myself that it was funny that a footballer had a bank card made for kids.

'Because they hadn't paid any money yet, we just kept them talking. I kept saying to him, "You are Wayne Rooney. I've seen you on the telly." But he kept telling us he was a boxer.

'Eventually, he laughed and admitted who he was. Almost immediately, he started bragging about it. He showed us photographs on his mobile phone of all the other Everton players. I was a bit star-struck.

'He was drinking a lot, and so were his mates. After about 40 minutes, the fair-haired lad came back with the money. As he gave the card back to Rooney, I asked whether I could see his name on it. It said "Rooney", and I was buzzing.

'It was a good job, because we were just about ready to leave, because we were beginning to think they were messing us about and were not going to pay us. I told Rooney, "You are a Premiership footballer; you must have money." Rooney then counted it out and Mark gave it to us.'

Charlotte was a bright girl and her memory recall was excellent. Almost without pausing for breath, she carried on describing the night's proceedings in minute detail. Her account was straightforward, and she didn't shy away from going into the awkward moments she often experienced in her line of work.

She added: 'Then we paired up. But there was only one bedroom. The other girl stayed in the living room with the bald guy, and Katie and I went into the bedroom with Rooney and Mark.

'We all got on the double bed, and I stripped down to my underwear. Katie stripped to just her bra. Rooney was naked but Mark left his T-shirt on. I started fondling Rooney.

'When I am working, I don't like to have sex in the same room in front of others, especially my sister, so I said this and Rooney suggested we go into the bathroom. It was a scruffy bathroom. It wasn't properly decorated and the peach paint was peeling off the walls. It needed a good cleaning, and the bin was tipped over and rubbish had spilled out. The tiles on the bathroom floor had paint splashed on them.

'In the bathroom, I took my bra and knickers off. I said to Rooney, "Where do you want me?" It was a tiny bathroom. We started to have sex on the floor, but there wasn't enough room. So Rooney suggested we stand up, and we had sex with me bending over the bath.

'It lasted about ten or fifteen minutes. I was laughing all the time, because I couldn't believe I was having sex with Wayne Rooney. He was laughing as well. He seemed to be enjoying it.

'I think he was turned on by the fact that I'm quite tall and I've got an athletic body. I stay in shape, I go the gym and, even though he was quite strong and rough, he couldn't throw me around.'

With the business of the evening taken care of, Rooney and the gang retired to the main bedroom for a bit of horseplay.

Charlotte said: 'Afterwards, we went back in the bedroom. Katie and Mark had finished and we all lay on the bed. Katie was messing about. Like me, she was star-struck with Wayne and asked if she could touch his willy, so that she could say she had held Rooney's manhood.

'But he couldn't get aroused. Like most men, he was turned on by the fact that we were twins. However, he had only just finished having sex with me and he was flat out. He was laughing. He just thought it was funny in the end.

'Then we all got dressed and went back in the living room.

'The fair-haired lad came out of the kitchen and joined us. We had been there about an hour and a half by that time. We were chatting, laughing and joking. Rooney was quite relaxed by then.

'I said in front of everyone, "I can't believe I've just shagged Wayne Rooney," and everyone laughed.

'Then I said that I needed something to prove it to all my mates, like his autograph. I couldn't believe it when he ripped the corner off a piece of paper that was lying around in the flat. It was a small piece, about 10 cm square. He was standing up and he rested the paper on the wall by the fireplace and started to write the message. I told him what to write just for a laugh. He was pissed and he did it. I couldn't believe he was so stupid to write that to a call girl. He couldn't write properly and didn't seem all that bright.

'I thought, "It's a good job he's a footballer."

'Katie and I would have stayed a bit longer but the other girl wanted to get away. We all left and they all stayed in the flat. I went home and told my mum, "I've kopped off with Wayne Rooney."

'She later found the note in my bedroom and I had to admit to her that I'd slept with him. But I didn't tell her I was an escort.'

In another conversation, Charlotte told me how Rooney had abused her on their second meeting. Her faced crumpled with humiliation as she recalled how angry Rooney had been with her after she refused his advances just four days after the bathroom romp. He called her a slag.

Fighting back the tears, Charlotte told me in her own words: 'On New Year's Day 2003, a few days after my first encounter with Rooney, I was in the Jolly Miller pub working behind the bar.

'Mark, one of the lads who had been at the party that first night, came in and recognised me. I was a bit embarrassed but he seemed nice and didn't make a big deal of me being an escort.

'He said that he was having a party at his flat again and invited me along.

'After work, at about midnight, I went to the flat and there was only this lad Mark there. I joked that he had asked me along just for sex but he said that Wayne Rooney and his mates would be along soon and he got on his mobile. I phoned Katie, because that made me feel safer.

'After about an hour, Rooney arrived with his mates and an older relative.

'Rooney was already wasted, clutching a bottle of Cristal champagne. He was wearing denim trainers, blue tracksuit bottoms and a grey T-shirt. He lay down, but after a while he sat up and started chatting.

'He was full of himself and sat between me and Katie and put his arms around us.

'I was a bit embarrassed that I'd been so star-struck last time so I was trying not to give him loads of attention, playing it cool.

'He expected me to be all over him and give him loads of compliments.'

Charlotte said that Rooney then asked her to go outside and sit in a car with him.

'At first, I said no, but his mates started to become nasty and aggressive towards me and Katie, treating us like dirt. One of them shouted at us when we turned the volume up on the stereo. So I said yes. It was a Ford, I think, but can't remember the colour because it was dark outside.

'I told him before we left that I was not having sex with him and that I was going just for a chat. But Rooney started trying it on. I said no, because deep down I felt dead cheap because of what happened the last time in the horrible bathroom.

'I felt sad inside that he knew I was just a prostitute and that's the way he'd look at me, no matter how nice or intelligent I was.

'When I knocked him back, he then offered me money. I felt ashamed and degraded that I was just a piece of meat. Surely I was entitled to some dignity? I'm only an ordinary girl who got into escorting to make ends meet and because I'd seen a programme on TV that made it look glamorous.

'I said, "No, just take me back to the flat."

'He said, "Please," and begged me – but I still said no. Then he called me a "fucking slag".

'We went back to the flat and he started kissing me at the door. I didn't react; I just looked at the floor. I had lost all my confidence and felt vulnerable. And then he exploded. He told me to "just fuck off".

'We went back up to the flat and his mates were being dead snotty. They were talking to us like shit. When they knew they weren't going to get anything, they just treated us like shit. So we decided to leave.'

But Charlotte's ordeal was not over yet. She was to receive a second dose of public humiliation from Rooney in a most unexpected place. Charlotte continued: 'A couple of months later, during the day, I was on my own in Liverpool queuing for a sandwich. Rooney was in front of me in the queue with some of his mates. He kept looking round at me, pointing and laughing. I thought he was bragging that's the girl I shagged over the bath and telling everyone that I was a prostitute. I didn't speak to him.

'Can you imagine how small I felt having to endure standing in the queue waiting for a salmon sandwich with him laughing?

'I hate him. During the Euro 2004 Championships, when everyone was making him out to be a saint, I thought, "If only you knew how nasty he was in real life."'

The story caused a big sensation, and the *Sunday Mirror* flew Charlotte and her sister off to Spain to keep them away from the rest of Fleet Street. When the dust had settled, they returned to Liverpool, gave up escorting by all accounts and settled down into college and their day jobs. On reflection, it was probably a bit naughty to deceive the girls, but they were well sorted out, and in the end the splash had the desired effect. The gangsters backed off.

WAYNE ROONEY: THE GANGSTERS MOVE IN

To be honest, I thought the story was a one-off. It turned out that it wasn't. Little did I know that all the while I'd been working on it I'd been surrounded by gangsters. I didn't realise this until the next big Rooney exposé.

2

Wayne Rooney: the Sex Tapes

About a month later, I travelled up from the *Sunday Mirror*'s London HQ to Liverpool once more, after a tip-off that Rooney was having sex with prostitutes again – this time in a back-street brothel. More standard Sunday-paper fare. But what made the story more desirable than most was the alleged presence of a juicy ingredient: that most valuable of Fleet Street commodities – good pictures. More accurately, CCTV footage allegedly showing England's biggest footy star in the act of visiting a brothel. Or, at least, that was what my tipster had heard. Newspapers love pictures because they solve two problems simultaneously. Photos and video-grabs are excellent proof that someone was somewhere at a particular time. You can't argue with them. Celebrities, and even their highly paid lying PRs, find it very difficult to talk their way out of compromising acts caught on film. Second, they illustrate the story – in short, they sell papers.

The first lead about Rooney's visits to a brothel had come to me about 18 months earlier, in the winter of 2002. A taxi-driver contact had called me to say that he knew a fellow cabbie who had witnessed Rooney being turned away from Liverpool's only 24-hour brothel, Diva's, more commonly known by its street address, 92 Aigburth Road. Taxi talk maybe, but this tipster was solid gold. He had recently given me a lead on a story about striker Robbie Fowler, then playing at Leeds, being attacked and robbed at his family home. In addition, this taxi driver had extensive contacts in the underworld, so his information was usually correct.

At the time of this first lead, Rooney was only 17 and had just burst onto the national stage after his life-changing, 25-yard shot to goal during an away game at Arsenal. After discussing the tip-off, the editor of the *Sunday Mirror* decided that it would be unfair to expose such precocious talent in a tabloid scandal for fear of a backlash from readers. She argued that if we ran the story, we risked alienating readers, who might criticise us for being too harsh on Rooney, arguing that he was only a young lad sowing his oats and too immature to understand what he was doing. Hard to believe, I know, but don't think everything you hear about tabloid journalists being *totally* ruthless is true. In addition, the editor feared the paper risked a further circulation-busting backlash from footy fans, who might attack the Trinity Mirror group for ruining the career of one of England's main hopes ahead of a big international tournament later that year.

There were also other factors. At the time, tabloid newspapers were being told to rein in their often extreme, exploitative treatment of celebrities, and more and more victims were claiming intrusion of privacy – and fighting back. Expensive lawyers were getting stuck in, asking where the public interest was in many of the celeb scandals that the papers ran. At the *Sunday Mirror*, we had to ask ourselves whether there was any real justification for turning over Roo. Second, Liverpool was a city that was particularly sensitive about the tabloid press, following *The Sun's* disastrous and shameful coverage of the Hillsborough disaster in which 96 Liverpool fans were killed in 1989. Exposing one of its favourite sons maliciously and for the wrong reasons might have resulted in an outcry. Our newspaper's holding company, Trinity, which controls the Mirror Group, also owns the flagship regional cash cow, the *Liverpool Echo*. The editor clearly had a number of responsibilities to consider. Consequently, the story was put on ice.

Meanwhile, I kept tabs on Rooney's misbehaviour in Liverpool, knowing that one day there would be justification. Following his heroic performance at the 2004 European Championship, Rooney's profile went stratospheric, but he continued to behave like the rootin'-tootin' scallywag he was.

Visiting prostitutes wasn't just a personal vice of Rooney's; it was a new trend amongst the city's teenagers – a social phenomenon. Many young lads from tough neighbourhoods like Norris Green and Croxteth were routinely visiting brothels in gangs of five and ten. This entertainment had firmly replaced traditional teenage pastimes such as going out boozing on Friday night and chatting up girls in bars. For the new generation of socially desensitised, third-generation, underclass hoodies, who demanded instant gratification on every level, going to a brasshouse for sex was as natural as carrying a gun or playing an Xbox in a skunk-filled room for eight hours a day. So many young scallies were now visiting brothels that it was not uncommon for Rooney to see different groups of lads he knew from around the barrio sitting in the waiting room. Consequently, rumours of his visits to prostitutes began to spread like wildfire. More people began to recognise him. I had calls from several sources, including businessmen, local journalists, other taxi drivers and students. I knew that it was only a matter of time before another newspaper got wind of the tip.

My original source called again to tell me that the word on the street was that Rooney had been captured on CCTV during visits to 92 Aigburth Road. Then my worst fears came true. I heard that rival newspapers, the *News of the World* and *The People*, had heard the rumours as well and had put 'watches' on the brothel – long-term surveillance using photographers with telephoto lenses hidden in blacked-out vans, usually lasting about one or two weeks at a time. They had also begun to ask tentative questions in the streets around the brothel to see if anyone knew anything.

During that time, the justification for a future scandal story landed in our laps. Rooney was now a massive name. He had performed outstandingly in Euro 2004 and was being billed as the next David Beckham. His childhood sweetheart Coleen McLoughlin was rapidly becoming a girl-next-door icon. And Rooney was poised to make his leap into the big, big-time with a transfer from Everton to any one of a string of clubs from all over the world who were queuing up to sign him.

Then he and his managers made a mistake. They sold the Rooney and Coleen story to *The Sun* and the *News of the World* newspapers for between £200,000 and £300,000. First, there was a massive public outcry in Liverpool at what they believed was a betrayal by Rooney in selling out to the Murdoch press – a boycott against *The Sun* newspaper for its treatment of Hillsborough victims was still in force. In disgust, many of the football fans, both of Liverpool and of Everton, who had been fiercely protective of their new prodigy now turned on Rooney. Before, when I had asked people who knew about Rooney's private life to comment, they had told me in no uncertain terms to 'fuck off'. No one was going to grass on one of their own. Now, enraged by a feeling that he had betrayed the Hillsborough dead, they were lining up to tell me every detail about his visits to prostitutes.

Second, there was now journalistic justification to begin a full-blown investigation into the story. In his world exclusive with *The Sun*, Rooney had boasted about his undying love for Coleen, implying that he was faithful and all the rest of it – clearly a fib that it was our duty to expose.

My mission now was to get my hands on the videotapes of Rooney in the brothel. That's if they existed, as at that time they were just a rumour. I felt no anxiety in undertaking this task. For a tabloid reporter, this was bread and butter. In ten years as a journalist, I had looked into stories about footballers taking drugs, losing it on booze-benders, playing away with Page 3 models, paying for sex, fighting, roasting female fans, rape, gang rape, sexual assault, groping lap-dancers, dogging, domestic violence, dealing drugs, drink-driving, gambling, attacking members of the public, underage sex, fraud, bribery, racism and generally every vice and crime under the sun that young, overpaid and often stupidly cocky lads could indulge in.

In addition to my experience, I had other advantages which could potentially give me an edge in standing this one up. I was born and brought up in Liverpool. I knew the lie of the land and had good contacts to help me track down the videotapes if they existed. I soon got a steer on a potential address connected to the madam who ran the brothel. I asked a colleague to go round to the house in the Formby area of Merseyside, but an old man who answered the door denied all knowledge. However, it was my gut instinct that this address was a flat used by the madam, or that this old man worked for the organisation and was just giving us the brush-off, as would anyone employed in a shady industry when reporters came knocking at the door. Whatever the truth, I wasn't going to waste time trying to get to the bottom of it, because it seemed like a one-step-removed lead anyway.

My second move was to go to the brothel and ask them for the tapes directly. Daft but sometimes effective. Diva's was located in a first-floor flat above a shopfront on Aigburth Road, a busy shopping area parallel to the banks of the River Mersey. The dual carriageway which the building faced was busy, a main thoroughfare from the southern suburbs, Speke docks and the industrial and commuter belt of Cheshire into the city centre. It was an ideal site for a cathouse, with lots of passing trade. The main entrance was around the side of the building in an alleyway which led into a street of red-brick, *Bread*-style Victorian terraced houses. The off-road entrance had been chosen for punter discretion and venue security. Brothels can be hothouses of crime and violence, by their nature attracting drunken and drug-crazed punters, sex pests, armed robbers intent on stealing the prostitutes' cash, protection racketeers and gangs of sex-crazed lads on stag nights – unpredictable undesirables of every description. Security is a priority. The working girls and the wedge they generate must be protected at all times. Ominously, the front door was guarded by locked iron gates and the buzzer was intercommed-up.

So far so good. However, before a job like this is approached, it is often important to consider the bigger picture and cover all the angles, ahead of making any bold moves. I began thinking through all the possible outcomes. The location of the brothel was significant and alarming at the same time. First of all, the brothel was situated less than half a mile away from a notorious street called Park Road at the heart of the city's underworld. Park Road was a run-down, shabby hill running through the dockside heartlands, and the maze of terraced streets around it had given rise to some of the most dangerous and wealthy gangsters not only in the UK but in the world. Coincidentally, I had lived in this area for the first few years of my life, and my family had retained close links.

The tough Dingle neighbourhood around Park Road had always had its fair share of crime, but the area's proximity to the docks, combined with its entrenched gangland culture, had given its mobsters a head start in the early days of drug-dealing during the '80s and '90s. To make matters worse, less than a mile away from Park Road, Granby Street was the main thoroughfare through the city's once riot-torn ghetto of Toxteth. A virtual no-go area for much of the '80s and early '90s, the street had made itself a key distribution point in the drugs trade in northern England.

Many of the crime families who had operated in places like Park Road and Granby Street had been there for between 50 and 100 years and were skilled in the arts of contraband smuggling and international-trade-based crime such as money-laundering, commercial burglary and corruption. In the early '80s, they applied their skills to drug-dealing, and a disproportionate number of them became multimillionaires. The superstar rogues' gallery included figures such as Curtis Warren, the wealthiest villain in British criminal history and *Sunday Times* Rich Listee, worth an estimated £200 million. Other narco luminaries included Colin Borrows, Britain's first crack-dealer, Tommy 'Tacker' Comerford, the heroin-baron boss of Britain's first drugs cartel as defined by HM Customs and Excise, and John Haase, the criminal mastermind who controlled the heroin-smuggling Turkish Connection and who ran guns countrywide as proficiently as the IRA.

Stood outside a back-street brothel on a warm summer's day, I came up with a few theories. With its proximity to the manors ruled by the local crime godfathers, this establishment and those who ran it were surely 'connected' – that is, related to gangsters. In addition, the brothel was just a couple of hundred yards away from a once-notorious, mob-controlled pub called Cheers. A battle for the right to use this '80s fun pub as a hang-out between a local family called the Ungis and a multi-millionaire black drug-baron called Johnny Phillips had resulted in one of the bloodiest episodes of gang warfare this country has ever seen. The place was nothing special, but the chrome, grey and pink bar had become a prized status symbol as a place to go for an after-hours drink, especially of a Sunday night. Local businessman and family leader David Ungi was slain in a Chicago-style gun feud, triggering scores of other shooting-related incidents. Rival Phillips, right-hand man of cocaine-lord Curtis Warren, died in mysterious circumstances later. Though the inquest did not conclude foul play, underworld sources maintain he was killed by a shadowy assassination gang called The Cleaners, a network of former-IRA gunmen turned contract executioners skilled in the dark arts of covert, undetectable killings.

Bearing this in mind, I decided to make a few calls to find out the lie of the land before I pressed the brothel's buzzer, just in case I went inside and never came out again. First, I made a call to an underworld contact, a very powerful international businessman who knew many of the villains from the area because he had grown up in these very same streets. The businessman confirmed my very worst fears. He told me that the brothel was under the 'protection' of a mob boss from a notorious crime family. The mob boss is known as The Pizzaman, because of his ability to deliver many aspects of organised crime, including contract killings, efficiently, and to your door, if necessary.

Though The Pizzaman was responsible for security, on a day-to-day basis the brothel was actually owned by an investor and run by an attractive former business professional who used a false name. Let's call her Blondie. After a spate of armed robberies and attacks, The Pizzaman had magnanimously decided to offer his security services to 'protect' the premises for a slice of the profits, knowing

35

that his reputation alone would deter most criminals from trying it on again.

This information gave me mixed feelings. On the one hand, villains do not like reporters meddling about in their shady business interests. On the other hand, major villains today are often media savvy. They understand that newspapers will pay big money for celeb sex-scandal stories and they will not often stand in the way of a business deal.

So I gave it a shot. I pressed the buzzer and asked to see the manageress. I was let in through the iron gates at the bottom of a narrow set of stairs. At the top of the stairs, there was another security door, protected by a second iron gate. Oh, dear! If I was trapped in the reception behind three locked doors and someone didn't like the look of me, there was little chance of getting out.

The lobby area was very claustrophobic. The receptionist told me that Blondie was not there, so I left my card and quickly got off. Before I did, I turned around to say goodbye and to look to see if the place was camera'd-up. Bingo! Above a doorway at the opposite end of the reception there was a single CCTV security camera. If it was real and well maintained, that meant the camera would get a good glimpse of the arrival of all visitors, so there was a chance that the legendary tapes actually existed.

Some time later, I got a call from another female employee. I told her that I was after the Wayne Rooney tapes. She told me that Rooney had never been to the brothel and denied their existence. I got the feeling she was lying, so I decided another tack. I drafted in an associate to pose as a freelance reporter to go back to the brothel to ask about the tapes independently of me. People who are not used to dealing with national newspapers sometimes feel less threatened by freelancers, especially in Liverpool, where tabloid reporters are seen in the same light as devil-worshipping paedophile serial killers. In addition, a freelancer often is perceived as being more 'impartial' than a staff reporter at a national newspaper, and 'punters' open up to them.

I told the associate not to reveal he was working for the *Sunday Mirror* but to imply he was working for another national newspaper all the same. This is a very basic but subtle scare tactic. The owners of the brothel would now believe that more than one newspaper knew about the story and would fear a news stampede. To prevent losing control of the situation and the prized asset, they might be forced to come to the negotiating table with me. The downside was the real risk of the story spreading – that the brothel might act unilaterally and contact other papers such as the *News of the World*, believing that the freelancer was representing them. Even worse for me, the brothel owners might panic and contact a PR guru like Max Clifford to instruct him to sell their story in a bidding war. But, knowing how secretive these people were, I banked on them dealing with what was in front of them – which was either me or the phoney freelancer controlled by me.

And that's exactly what they did. Soon, the fake freelancer reported back that the brothel had confirmed Rooney's sex sessions and that he had been videoed arriving and leaving the brothel. Excellent news. From here on in, it should have been a textbook operation – a simple case of getting the cheque book out, buying the tapes from whoever owned them and interviewing the prostitutes who had slept with Rooney. I pictured myself writing up the story, seeing my old nan on the way back to Lime Street train station and getting off back to London as soon as.

How wrong I was. From that moment on, the gangsters moved in – with terrifying consequences. Several rival mobsters got wind of our intent to buy the videotapes and joined in the race. The front-runners included:

1. The Blackmailer

The Blackmailer was a leading member of a ruthless drug-dealing gang based in north Liverpool. He specialised in 'taxing' rival drug-dealers of their super-profits by torturing them. He had recently moved into taxing Premiership footballers by threatening to expose their sexual indiscretions. One of his first victims included a Liverpool player. And since then he had gone from strength to strength, extorting cash from several leading footballers. The Blackmailer was intent on stealing the Rooneygate tapes before or after they were handed over to the *Sunday Mirror* in order to force Rooney or his agents to stump up hundreds of thousands of pounds to keep them out of the press.

2. The Extortionist

The Blackmailer's rival, who had the same plan.

3. The Security Boss

A well-respected security consultant. The Security Boss hoped to endear himself to the Rooney clan by offering his services as a feared underworld fixer to get the tapes back and hand them safely over to them. Doing favours for rich footy players was a way of getting them onside in the hope of landing a lucrative contract as a bodyguard. Rooney had no knowledge that this man was acting in his interests, nor is he related to any of Rooney's security staff.

4. The Evertonian

An underworld boss and fanatical Everton supporter who vowed to kill anyone who interfered with Wayne's form – including tabloid reporters – in order to keep him on the ball at Everton FC and give him no excuse to leave.

5. The Con Man

A specialised con artist pretending to be employed by Rooney and his lawyer as an inquiry agent.

Each gangster wanted to get his hands on the tapes for his own reasons, all of them involving money, because, at the end of the day, the subject involved was a Premiership star with bags of it. This may have been a seedy affair, a back-street brothel in a poor part of Liverpool, but everyone understood that what was at stake was the future of the potentially richest football player in the UK. Millions of pounds of sponsorship money hung in the balance.

The task ahead was daunting. Not only was I faced with the difficult job of negotiating the tapes out of the hands of the brothel owners and their lawyers, but I would have to negotiate a safe path through the minefield of potential threats, beatings and injuries.

First up came The Blackmailer. Through a mutual contact, a phone message was passed to me. 'When you get the tapes, don't give them to your newspaper, give them to us. We'll sell them back to Wayne. He'll be made up and we'll give you 50 per cent.' Of course, they knew I could not be bought, but they were giving it a try anyway, in the hope that we'd all be mates. During my career, I had only ever been offered one bribe before. It happened when I was a young reporter and was covering a case of a bent solicitor accused of rape. In the lift on the way up to the court, he silently pulled out a wad of notes and explained in sign language (in case he was being taped) that it was £200 and that it was mine if I left and did not cover his case.

In Liverpool, the gangsters knew I was beyond reproach, but the offer of a slice of a blackmail deal was their opening gambit. A polite and everyday occurrence to them. Not even a shot across the bows.

A few days later, another call came through from the middleman. 'If you don't cooperate, then they'll just find you and take the tapes off you.' The middleman tried to explain that it was easier for me just to get onside with them because there were dark forces at play prepared to stop at nothing, that I had kids, etc. I refused again.

Meanwhile, I had made contact with Blondie, and the *Sunday Mirror* had made an initial offer of £30,000 for the tapes. This was immediately rejected. The second offer was £50,000. But as they pondered the readies, a fresh danger to the story came in from the wings: the appearance on the scene of the *News of the World*. As well as the brothel and the gangsters, this variable was a headache I could do without. The *News of the World* had dispatched one of their best operators to the field of battle, a northern editor based in Leeds ominously known as the Prince of Darkness. The

FOOTBALL AND GANGSTERS

Prince of Darkness had been tipped off about the story by a junior executive at the *Liverpool Echo*, who had put two and two together based on our presence in the city and little requests for information here and there from my team. For his help on the story, the junior executive was later rewarded with a staff job at the *News of the World*.

Prince of Darkness or not, he wasn't getting the story. The appearance of a bidding rival on the scene inevitably meant we would have to pay more for the story than if we were competing against ourselves, but that was manageable if we got the story. Immediately, I instructed another colleague to keep an eye on the *News of the World* reporter. His movements were monitored more or less from the moment he arrived at Liverpool's Crown Plaza hotel until he left – without their story, by the way.

Anyway, a more serious threat appeared on the scene in the form of a second gangster, known as The Extortionist, whose real name cannot be given, for legal reasons. An underworld contact warned me that The Extortionist had been chasing the videotapes for a long time in the hope of taxing Wayne Rooney for between £100,000 and £500,000. He was furious that we had interrupted his scheme and warned that we either pull out, hand over the vids once we got them or face the consequences. I decided that we'd have to take option three, and I made it known through the underworld grapevine that no one was having the tapes except us.

However, on that score, the trail suddenly went dead. Blondie and her associates at the brothel stopped returning my calls. This was very worrying. Either the *News of the World* had whisked her off to a hotel with the vids or the gangsters had got their way. Either way, the wheels were coming off our operation fast and we had to find out why.

We put a watch on the brothel. No one significant turned up, just a steady stream of expectant punters. They were in for a letdown, because Blondie had ordered the brothel to be temporarily closed to protect the staff from gangsters and reporters. Clearly, both Blondie and The Pizzaman were staying away. We contacted The Pizzaman direct by phone for the first time, but he played it super cool, denying that he had any involvement in the brothel. We told him that, whether he was or wasn't in charge, he should get a message to Blondie to get in touch. Twenty-four hours later, there was still no sign.

I then instructed the freelancer to go into the brothel and leave a message. At this point, things turned nasty. It became apparent that The Pizzaman had put our watch under counter-surveillance. They were watching us watching them. Most drug-dealers are schooled in the dark arts of counter-surveillance – an almost natural instinct to them. Ominously, two heavies began taking pictures of our fake freelancer, and when he moved off they began following in a green car at close quarters. Even after two or three miles of dense traffic, they were still on his tail, determined and alarming. It wasn't clear at this stage whether they were just trying to freak him out or they were going to drag him out of the car in a quiet place and do him in. I instructed the freelancer to get into the city centre and seek sanctuary in the Moat House hotel. They wouldn't assault him in public like that. But, more importantly, and completely unknown to the hotel's owners and staff, this was a meeting place for some of the most serious and heavyweight 'community leaders' in the city. And they would not be pleased about an uncouth attack on a helpless reporter disturbing their mid-afternoon cups of tea. In the meantime, I arranged for backup security to make sure nothing bad happened to the reporter.

The Pizzaman was playing a typical game of criminal double-bluff. I knew deep down that he wanted to sell the tapes to us, but in the underworld he would be considered a grass if he cooperated with Her Majesty's press. So this was a show for everyone in the underworld to see. The message to Rooney and all of the gangsters who were now chasing the tapes was 'I am The Pizzaman. I am a hardened criminal. There is no way in the fucking world that I would sell a story to those dirty bastard papers. In fact, if they come near me, I'll have them bashed up.' He was clearly being approached by other villains, possibly The Blackmailer and The Extortionist, who were offering him money for tapes or at least trying to make a partnership deal with him. So he was weighing up his options. Who would give the most money: blackmailers or the papers? If he went with the blackmailers, would that upset the pro-Rooney villains, including The Security Boss and The Evertonian? It was a minefield of gangster politics made even madder by the presence of two powerful Fleet Street newspapers.

The coded message specifically to us was 'Never contact me directly. If you want to buy the tapes, then you'll have to deal direct with Blondie, who is fronting this deal for me.' OK, fair enough, but Blondie was nowhere to be seen and our patience was running out. Either way, it meant another day sat in the hotel room waiting for the mobile to ring, eating room-service prawn sarnies, drinking tea with only *Trisha* and *Sky News* for comfort, and still no contact. At this point, we had no time to play games with villains such as The Pizzaman full of prison sly.

A full-frontal attack was called for. The pretend freelancer approached The Pizzaman directly. Bravely, he visited his shop on Park Road. An assistant told him that The Pizzaman wasn't in but they could contact him if he'd like to wait. Minutes later, an anonymous Ford saloon pulled up and a beefy man in a black leather jacket jumped out. He walked quickly into the shop, got hold of the freelancer and threw him over the counter. The freelancer was roughed up, threatened, dark words were exchanged and he was sent packing.

The next day, Blondie called up screaming and shouting about our direct approach and claiming that The Pizzaman was now blaming her for the mess. Whatever the truth, relieved that she had finally resumed contact, we upped our bid to £70,000 to compensate her for her troubles and keep her sweet. She got herself a local lawyer and then started playing the *Sunday Mirror* and the *News of the World* off against each other in an old-fashioned Fleet Street bun fight.

The bids quickly surpassed £100,000. Meanwhile, the feeding frenzy further whetted the appetite of the underworld, who now believed that the tapes must be even more sensational than first thought and consequently that the blackmail fees could be upped. Still, none of the bidders knew what was really in them. We were all bidding blind. Both I and other members of the team were threatened.

We were staying at the Woolton Redbourne Hotel, one of the city's best-kept secrets, which has now closed down. The Redbourne was a centuries-old, country-style manor secreted in a wealthy suburb of Liverpool, favoured by football stars and visiting celebrities. Joan Collins had stayed there. Gerard Houllier, the Liverpool FC supremo at the time, used the private dining rooms to hold his weekly management meeting discussing team tactics. I'd watched a newly signed Premiership player escort two high-class prostitutes – who had been flown in from Paris especially for the occasion – to one of the suites. In the guest book, Gazza had written a daft message about the reality TV show *Big Brother*. I chose the Redbourne Hotel to be my team's HQ during this long and difficult investigation because the staff could be trusted to be discreet and keep an eye out for our security.

It didn't take long for the gangsters to find out where we were staying. More threats, more moody calls, more jumpy nerves. I needed someone who could watch our backs – not a bodyguard or bouncer, someone less ontop than that, but who could get busy if necessary. If it got as far as fisticuffs, in my view, we had failed. We had to stay one step ahead of everyone who was on our case – be sharper, sneakier and faster. I needed someone who could be our eyes and ears, constantly on the lookout for signs of an attack, who could weigh up an underworld threat within seconds and deal with it.

There are several types of professional who specialise in this type of counter-surveillance. There's your former-SAS type, undoubtedly the best in the world at what he does, but some of them – not all – find it difficult to operate in the underworld. There's your private detective and professional bodyguard – good, but only up to a point. Finally, there's the former villain, who knows all the tricks – the poacher turned gamekeeper who is able to think in exactly the same way as the crooks whose presence he is there to detect, good simply because he was once a gangster himself.

FOOTBALL AND GANGSTERS

Former villains are often sensitive to a range of threats. The two great fears in a drug-dealer's life are a) being caught by the police and/or Customs and Excise and b) being attacked and robbed by rival gangs. That means former criminals are familiar with formal, law-enforcement-style surveillance as well as the more street-level but equally effective tactics used by 'tie-up' gangs – specialist criminal cells who prey on other gangs with extreme, blood-curdling violence. A combination of criminal mentality, experience and prison cunning often makes reformed gangsters excellent counter-surveillance operatives.

The Turk is a reformed heroin-trafficker who specialises today in carrying out certain 'specialist' work. As a leading member of the Turkish Connection – the world's leading opium-trafficking network – The Turk had spent years dodging law-enforcement officers in a dozen countries until he was outwitted by HM Customs' crack MI5-boosted Lima 3 team and spent years in a British jail. Fresh out of the shovel, penitent and lightning quick of mind, he was ideal for the job. The bonus ball was that The Turk's main customers during his reign as Britain's number-one druglord were the Liverpool mafia. He had the measure of the Scouse gangsters on our case and even knew some of them personally.

The Turk didn't sleep much. Stealthily, he roamed the grounds of the hotel. He scoured the perimeter, the adjacent buildings and the surrounding roads. Within hours of his appointment, he had unearthed his first catch. He discovered three men hiding in the bushes in a patch of woodland opposite the hotel car park. From his bedroom window, he had watched these camouflaged sleuths watching us in the early hours through to the morning. To test their intentions, he drove his anonymous hire car out onto the streets and, sure enough, got followed. In his opinion, the men in the bushes were villains hoping to ambush us or burgle our rooms in the hope of stealing the videotapes, which, at that point, we did not have but they obviously believed we did.

Later that day, the team, including me, moved rooms to a more secure, self-contained wing of the hotel called the Coach House, which was equipped with a coded entry system. It meant that we could all be in a sealed-off part of the hotel in which no other guests were allowed, making it more difficult for anyone to get at us.

After relocating, I left the hotel in my car to go to a meeting. The Turk left separately a short while later to see if anyone was following me. Sure enough, there was a green hatchback on my tail. I couldn't see who was in it, but we managed to lose them at a busy roundabout called the Wavertree clock tower.

The tape auction continued. The *Sunday Mirror* and the *News of the World* were head to head, matching each other's bid at every round in bouts of head-spinning Fleet Street muscle-flexing. This was going to break the bank if we weren't careful. The bids eventually burst through the threshold authorised by the editor. She had to go to a senior board member to get any further bids signed off. This was getting serious. I had the feeling that, depending on who won the bidding wars, either the Trinity Mirror shareholders or Rupert Murdoch would not be pleased when the bill arrived.

Eventually, The Pizzaman had to start taking counsel from people who knew how the media operated. He needed to know things like which paper was the easiest to do business with, which one would try to rip him off, whether anyone in the underworld had dealt with newspapers like this before and what tricks he should look out for. Calls flooded in to The Pizzaman and his brothers from extremely powerful underworld figures from literally all over the world. Some of these international figures were worth tens of millions of pounds, with interests ranging from building supplies to electronics, but their power base remained on the streets of UK cities. They included expat villains in Europe and deal-makers doing business in the Far East. One of the most influential phoned The Pizzaman and said simply, 'Go with them. Go with the *Sunday Mirror*. Go with Graham Johnson. He will take care of you. He has a good reputation for keeping his word.' That short reference meant it was a done deal at that point. That was all the reassurance The Pizzaman needed to put his trust in me and the *Sunday Mirror*.

The *News of the World* knew nothing of this, of course, so it was a coincidence shortly afterwards when they dropped out of the running somewhere just above the £100,000 mark, citing poverty. The Prince of Darkness began to make preparations to leave Liverpool. He was no longer on this story. We had him under secret surveillance. He had eggs for breakfast before checking out of the Crown Plaza hotel near the Liver Building at about 8.30 a.m., bound for his regional office in Leeds. We followed him to the outskirts of the city, just to make sure he wasn't double-bubbling us in some way. *News of the World* reporters are notoriously good and very, very cunning. So we had to keep an eye on him until we thought he was no longer a threat.

Blondie then agreed to show us a copy of the videotapes at the office of her solicitor in Liverpool as a taster of what we were buying. Coincidentally, I knew the lawyer. He was a close pal. But he acted purely professionally and did not give us any special privileges. We had to sign an industry-standard confidentiality agreement prohibiting us from using any of the material without first coming to a formal financial agreement with her. The video showed Rooney visiting the brothel on two separate occasions. The first one showed him arriving with a young Liverpool player. Rooney goes into a waiting room, takes his shoes off and falls asleep, while his pal strips off in anticipation of what is to come. The Liverpool player is seen walking around the reception naked, masturbating in preparation and chatting up the bored receptionist.

He then goes first for a 30-minute sex session with a prostitute dressed as a cowgirl. But there is an unfortunate interruption. During the romp, the police call at the brothel, a routine check to make sure everything is OK. However, everyone thinks it's a police raid. The cowgirl runs topless from the room, quickly followed by the naked Liverpool player clutching his clothes.

After the police leave, both the cowgirl and the Liverpool player go back into the room to finish off. Second up is England and Everton star Wayne Rooney. He is woken from his doze and casually saunters into the room carrying his shoes in his hand. He emerges with the cowgirl a short while later.

On the second visit, Rooney arrives at the brothel with five or six football pals, mostly Liverpool and Everton players. The receptionist does not allow them in because she says Rooney is too young and the gang, clearly fresh from a night on the booze, are too rowdy. They are stopped from entering by a steel, cage-like security gate at the top of the stairs. The gang embark on a 15-minute rant in which desperate Rooney offers the receptionist cash for sex and another het-up player threatens to masturbate on the stairs. The receptionist holds firm and they are directed to another brothel.

In truth, both videos were kind of underwhelming – grainy, bad quality and not actually showing Roo scoring between the red satin sheets of the 'heart room'. But as evidence they were dynamite, and it was all systems go. We then moved on to a protracted round of contractual negotiations between Blondie's lawyer in Liverpool and Mirror lawyers in Canary Wharf over issues such as copyright.

While these finer details were being sorted out, we were not allowed to remove copies of the tapes from the solicitor's office. Blondie still wanted more money and the holding arrangement was that we would not be allowed to have a copy of our own until a final figure was agreed upon. The private viewing had given us an opportunity to see exactly what we were buying, so the editor and her bosses could make a proper cost evaluation of it, as up to that point we had been bidding blind.

In the meantime, more rats had smelled out the possibility of making some money and joined in the fray. A group of infamous con men had got wind of a rumour that Wayne Rooney, his agents and his lawyers had employed private detectives to get their hands on the tapes before we did. True or not, the plan was a perfectly legitimate course of action, and inquiry agents are often used by celebrities when they are in trouble. It was something that we were expecting. One seemingly genuine investigator had approached one of our reporters outside his hotel trying to get him onside. Another had put in a blag call to the freelancer in the hope of luring him to a meeting in Manchester where he would be offered big exclusives in exchange for dropping the Rooney story.

However, we were not expecting phoney PIs: con men impersonating inquiry agents. One known as The Con Man approached a source close to the story, offering huge sums of money for the tapes once they had formally been handed over to us. The silver-tongued rogue then tried to wheedle sensitive information out of the source. His partner began asking for the email addresses of *Sunday Mirror* reporters, presumably with the intention of hacking into them to dig out secret communications with their newsdesk. Fortunately, I was then tipped off about the phoney PIs, and when we distanced ourselves, cutting off all ties with their source, they revealed their true colours by becoming violent and abusive. We had no option but to ignore them and get on with the job in hand.

Blondie continued to bargain hard, squeezing even more money out of Trinity Mirror's shell-shocked execs, even though we were the only ones in the running. Her technique was simple but effective: 'Now that the *News of the World* are out the way, either you give me more dough or these tapes are going in the River Mersey.' She had Britain's biggest newspaper group between a rock and a hard place. She was banking on the fact that journalists are more desperate for a good story than a £50,000-a-week footy player is for sex with an old granny. She had dealt with a lot of over-desperate types in her time – she knew the psychology back to front. Eventually, the *Sunday Mirror* settled on a six-figure sum with Blondie and finally publication was in sight.

The lawyers set to work drawing up a formal contract containing the final figure. In the meantime, Blondie generously handed over copies of the video in good faith, knowing that they could not be used without her permission, as laid down in the initial confidentiality agreement. Even though the final contract was not complete during this period of transition, she was still covered by the first agreement. This is a good device which allows all aspects of the process to continue while formalities are being completed.

As an additional measure to protect her interests, Blondie insisted that the original 30-hour security tape be copied so that we could work off the duplicates and she could retain the master. She also took the precaution of insisting that the copies be edited slightly. Specifically, she demanded that the identities of some of the people on the tape – mainly punters and members of staff not directly involved in the story – be disguised.

This was a logistically complicated operation. We had to take the tapes to a secure edit suite in Lancashire and have the face of each prohibited person 'blobbed' digitally. That meant putting a black strip across the head of each person in question. Blondie insisted that her right-hand man be present during the process to make sure it was done thoroughly and that no sneaky unblobbed copies were made by us. When it was completed, Blondie allowed us to keep some CD and VHS copies of the original.

Security-wise, the initial editing process was a bonus for us. It meant that the handover of copies from them to us took place at a secret location well outside of Liverpool, under two sets of watchful eyes, namely our *Sunday Mirror* investigators and Blondie's right-hand man. It reduced the risk of the tapes and CDs being stolen and allowed us time to make plans for their dispersal into the hands of the reporters and photographers who would put the story together. That way, no one would be likely to be mugged for them.

However tedious and long-winded this process was, it was clear that the project was moving in the right direction as far as the *Sunday Mirror* was concerned. For the gangsters, that spelled doom. Their dreams of a big sting were rapidly fading into the distance. Consequently, some of the villains began to get more and more desperate as they saw the prize drifting away from them. Dirty tricks increased. One day, a stunningly beautiful blonde lady appeared at the door of the hotel. She was wearing a very revealing top and a very short skirt. She looked very out of place – it was early afternoon in a sleepy suburban hotel. She brushed past reception, mentioned the name of a *Sunday Mirror* investigator and walked straight up to his room. Clearly, she had been briefed about what room he was in. The woman was obviously a prostitute.

Evidently, this was an attempt to compromise one of the investigators on the *Sunday Mirror* team in a classic honeytrap, or to get someone into his room to search it for the tapes. Luckily, our basic security measures had paid off. Days earlier, we had all moved rooms to the Coach House but left several rooms in the main hotel under our names as a decoy. These rooms were empty, and consequently the honeytrap blonde had not got in. She strutted out of the hotel like Kate Moss on the catwalk, having to run the gauntlet of me and the team, who were stood around in the lobby or sat in the cars looking on in awe. She could see us, obviously, but it was apparent that she had not been given our descriptions because she seemed to have no idea who we were. We watched in stunned silence from a few feet away as she smiled and coolly slipped into the back seat of a minicab.

Negotiations continued over the draft contract until it started to look like something The Beatles had signed with EMI and their own label, Apple Records. Blondie was not daft, and she was protecting herself with an encyclopedia of small print – too much, to be fair, but she would not be persuaded otherwise. But even worse was the unexpected arrival of a new player in the game. A well-respected hard-man known as The Security Boss had taken it on himself – without the knowledge of Wayne Rooney – to act on the player's behalf. The Security Boss was a young member of an old-school gangster family who had ruled Liverpool with an iron fist in their day. The family had once been allied to the crime family of which The Pizzaman was joint head. The Security Boss reasoned that if he could lean on The Pizzaman to stop the story from going ahead, then he would be able to use this show of loyalty and muscle as a bargaining chip to win a much-desired security contract with the cash-rich Premiership star. Personally, The Security Boss had no bad intentions towards us or Rooney – but he had the reputation and respect to make The Pizzaman think twice about the big deal which Blondie was fronting for him. And, at the end of the day, if he didn't get what he wanted, then it could all turn very nasty.

The intervention was badly timed for us. Though the contracts were well on the way to being completed, crucially we had not yet signed on the bottom line. We couldn't even run a preview version of the story, known in the trade as a spoiler, because of the confidentiality agreement which we'd signed. Blondie and The Pizzaman could walk away at any moment and we would be left swinging. Legally, our tapes would be as good as useless.

The Security Boss was applying serious pressure to The Pizzaman, and he had to listen. Both were heavyweights, and The Pizzaman knew that if he went ahead with the *Sunday Mirror* deal, it meant serious disrespect to The Security Boss – meaning possible gangwar. Men had been killed and maimed for a lot less. Both men understood that. Each of them had lost family members and friends to guns and violence, and now a grainy video of Wayne Rooney sauntering through a brothel carrying his designer shoes was threatening to plunge the whole caboodle into yet more gang violence. That is the power of modern football.

The Security Boss also made it known that he had put a team on us with instructions to get the tapes back. His men were searching the city as he negotiated with The Pizzaman over a cup of tea. His patience was running out, and he let it be known that if he found the *Sunday Mirror* reporters, they were in for serious trouble. That was the official word on the street. It wasn't personal; it was just business.

Word got to us that all over the city enquiries were being made, hotels and pubs were being searched. Our security measures had been paying off so far, as doors weren't quite being booted in yet, but it wouldn't be long before either I or one of the team was going to be rolled up in a carpet and put in the boot of a car on the way to a pre-prepared torture abode. One underworld ally called to warn me cryptically: 'They are going to cop for you, mate. You're going in the boot of a car, no two ways about it. You'll only realise how foolish you have been when the only thing you can smell is the petrol.' I took it that he had been in the boot of a car before and was referring to the overwhelming odour of fuel from the spare can or the tank.

I felt like saying: 'I'm only a tabloid reporter, and this is only a daft story about a daft kid being caught shagging a prostitute. There is definitely no need for all this fuss.' But that was a perception ten years out of date. This was not just a silly kiss and tell – this was modern football, millions of pounds were at stake and every rat in town wanted a piece. So far, I had The Blackmailer, The Extortionist, The Security Boss, The Evertonian and The Con Man on my case – and I was heading for a tight space next to a petrol can, according to the pal. I had to start making some decisions. I declared to my team that the situation was now officially bang ontop. In fact, it was worse than that; it was ontop to death, and evasive action had to be taken at once.

We split up. I went to the Carriage Works hotel in the city centre along with the phoney freelancer, who later moved again to the Holiday Inn Express near the Albert Dock as an additional measure. The Turk moved into a quiet boutique hotel near the Liver Building. His nocturnal habits, plus a series of oddly tense visits from his contacts, caused the owner to burst into tears. Others went to the Moat House and the SAS Radisson, and a backup room was booked at a cheap motel on the Dock Road.

Finally, the contracts were completed. Both parties signed, and we were now free to run the story. I started analysing the videotapes and CD copies, transcribing every cough and spit from the hissy but often comical soundtrack and logging every event on the footage in preparation for filing the story. Sounds easy, but it's a logistical nightmare formatting it onto other CDs, organising more copies, sending them off to electronics experts for visual and audio enhancement, etc. But the story had to be filed quickly before someone got hurt or the whole exposé came crashing down. Luckily, we got away with it by the skin of our teeth, and the words and pics were pinged down to London in good time for the newsdesk and the sub-editors to work their magic.

In the meantime, the editor was busy negotiating with Wayne Rooney's PR people, convincing them that there was no point in injuncting the story, as the evidence was overwhelming and if they prevented publication this week it would only go in next week. The only winners would be the lawyers on double-triple-time wages for getting a judge out of bed on a Saturday morning to sign the paperwork.

Rooney's PR guru Ian Monk is among the best in the world. As a former *Daily Mail* journalist, he knows when to let it go. Instead, he concentrated on extracting a few face-saving concessions (for his red-faced client) out of the editor in exchange for a confessional statement. In simple terms, instead of denying it, Rooney admitted to the lot. This gave the paper a comfort zone. Everybody was happy. To further reduce the risk of injunction, and, in fairness, to save the blushes of several of Rooney's pals, whom there was no justification in exposing, the names of the other Liverpool and Everton players involved were disguised.

On 22 August 2004, the story was run over the first six pages of the *Sunday Mirror*. On the front page, there was a massive video-grab picture of grinning Wayne Rooney inside the brothel next to the headline 'WORLD EXCLUSIVE: ROO IN A VICE DEN'. The main thrust of the story was that Rooney had sex with a string of hookers at the brothel, including a mother-of-six who dressed as a cowgirl, a kinky-boot-wearing brunette called Gina and a 48-year-old grandmother known as The Auld Slapper, who wore a rubber catsuit when they had sex.

Faced with the overwhelming evidence, Rooney confessed, or 'coughed' as it is known in the trade. In a statement through Ian Monk, the teenager said that he had been foolish to visit the parlour. He put it down to his young age and tried to say that the indiscretions took place before he had settled down with Coleen – perhaps a little white PR fib, which the newspaper was prepared to overlook in exchange for a much-wanted confession.

The admission was a great relief for us. It appeased the newspaper's lawyers, assuring them that they were doubly-safe in publishing the story, and it sent a message from the Rooney camp that they would not spring a last-minute injunction to prevent publication. In effect, they were swallowing the story. The statement read:

> It was at a time when I was very young and immature and before I had settled down with Coleen. I now regret it deeply and just

hope that people will understand that it was the sort of mistake
you make when you are young and stupid.

The story's devilish humour was in the detail. For instance, it told how
during one visit Rooney had not tried to hide his identity, even though
his boy-next-door image is worth £3 million to him in sponsorship
alone. In fact, he spent one visit signing autographs in the waiting room
while word spread by text message that he was inside. A gang of 30 fans
soon gathered outside, loudly chanting his name.

Most remarkable of all, Rooney came within an inch of being nabbed
by police in a spot-check on the 'massage parlour'. But even though the
police were ringing the bell, dozy Rooney was fast asleep on a sofa in the
waiting room, waiting for his turn with a prostitute.

The tapes also showed Rooney and a gang of friends – including two
Liverpool players who were not named in the story, for legal reasons
– getting turned away from the brothel after another visit following a
drunken night out. The players shouted abuse at the receptionist: 'We
don't care about the cameras. Put us in the paper.'

In desperation, Rooney added: 'I'll shag you for 50 quid.'

More often than not on these visits, though, he was allowed in. And
his favourite girl was a mixed-race Caribbean model called Amy, who
wore pink designer lingerie and high heels. He also had sex with another
hooker wearing a lacy basque and black hold-up stockings.

One of the most startling visits was captured on the 90-minute tape
that had been so hard to get. The antics with the busty blonde cowgirl
were comic, to say the least. The footage begins with Rooney and a pal,
an anonymous Liverpool star, arriving at the brothel. The blow-by-blow
order of events is as follows:

2.00 a.m. Door buzzer goes.

Receptionist: 'Have you been here before?'

Rooney: 'Yes.'

Friend: 'Yes.'

The players are let in. Rooney is dressed in a smart black zip-up jacket and dark trousers. His friend is wearing a grey tracksuit. Another punter walks into the reception area.

Punter: 'All right, kid.'

Rooney: 'All right, lad.'

Punter: 'What are you doing in these places, lad?'

Rooney: 'What? [Laughs] Same as you, lad.'

Cowgirl goes into the waiting room to introduce herself to the men, then goes away to get ready. Rooney's friend is shown into a room for sex. But he is impatient, and emerges in just his boxer shorts to see how long the cowgirl is going to be.

2.18 a.m. Cowgirl goes into the room wearing a black cowboy hat, black vest top and a black miniskirt, with black gloves up to the elbow and black cowboy boots. She is holding a small black bag containing condoms. She grabs a white towel and slams the door shut.

2.25 a.m. Police patrol buzz on the intercom. Receptionist knocks on the bedroom door to alert the cowgirl and Rooney's friend.

Receptionist: 'Get dressed! The police are here.'

Cowgirl comes running out of the sex room topless, wearing just her knickers and boots and carrying her cowboy hat in her right hand. Receptionist goes downstairs to speak to police. Rooney's friend swaggers out of the sex room half-dressed, holding his trainers. Receptionist returns.

Receptionist: 'It's all right. They've gone.'

Cowgirl apologises to Rooney and his friend.

Cowgirl (to Rooney, not realising he has fallen asleep on the sofa): 'I nearly had a heart attack there.'

2.30 a.m. The Liverpool player goes back into sex room. Cowgirl follows.

2.45 a.m. Receptionist knocks on the door to let them know that time is up.

2.53 a.m. Cowgirl emerges from the room laughing.

Friend: 'You're gorgeous you, babe.'

2.56 a.m. Receptionist goes into the waiting room to tell the still-sleeping Rooney that it's his turn. She wakes him up and he picks up his shoes and walks into the sex room after handing over his £10 entrance fee plus £35 for the 'full service'.

3.15 a.m. Cowgirl in full costume goes in to have sex with Rooney.

3.25 a.m. Rooney comes out of the sex room fully dressed after having sex and joins his friend in waiting room.

3.30 a.m. They leave.

Rooney: 'Tara! See you!'

Receptionist: 'Tara!'

The rest is pop-culture history: Rooney leaves; brothel sells tapes to the paper; paper's sales go up.

And to assist in this last little detail, I sent in an additional Rooneygate kiss and tell that was printed inside the paper. This was based on the account of a very experienced prostitute called Gina McCarrick, who had spoken to me accompanied by one of the brothel's receptionists. She told me in no-nonsense terms how Wayne Rooney had paid £45 to have sex with her. She wasn't at all star-struck during her liaison with soccer's boy wonder. To her, he was just another John. In fact, as he went for gold, all she could think about was which Pot Noodle she would have for supper on her break later that night. I was struck by how completely unfazed the 37-year-old veteran sex worker was by anything that happened in her massage boudoir. She told me, 'I love Pot Noodles and was thinking what flavour to have: chicken and mushroom or beef and tomato. I always have one on my break, and I just wanted him to finish so I could put the kettle on.'

Gina also told me that Rooney had asked her to wear a schoolgirl's uniform. But she made him make do with a '60s-style outfit of white PVC knee-high boots, black miniskirt and a black-and-white crop top which she already had on and couldn't be bothered changing. She then let me in on the gory details of the night's proceedings: 'Wayne was second up. One of his mates had gone first. In the room, there was a king-sized bed and mirrors on the wall. It's called the Red Room, because it's all red like a heart. It's meant to be romantic but a turn-on as well.

There's a coat-hanger rail and Wayne had already stripped off and hung his clothes on it. He was lying on the bed naked except for a gold chain around his neck. He knew the drill because he'd been here before – it was obvious. I knew that from gossip from other girls anyway. I looked good in full make-up – eyeliner, eyeshadow, foundation, blusher, lipstick – just like I was going to a nightclub.

'He was already lying on his belly, so I took my top off and my white Wonderbra. He could see my reflection in the mirror. I got on the bed and started body-to-body massaging him by rubbing my breasts all over him. It was an erotic massage, and Wayne groaned, showing his appreciation. He had a face like a smacked arse, and, although he was a bit chubby with a little belly on him, I could feel his muscles.

'After the massage, I gave him a slap on the bum and told him to roll over. He was aroused, definitely. Let's put it that way. There were a few little grunts. He was showing that he was turned on. Then I put a condom on him with one hand. Then I gave him oral sex. I was wondering how long it would take him to climax. I always try to make clients climax through oral sex because it saves me from having full sex. With the young lads, you know they are just going to pound you to death, and you want to get it over with before that happens. After about eight or nine minutes of oral sex, I said to Wayne, "Are you ready for sex now?"

'He said, "Yeah."

'Then I jumped off the bed to get in position. I do this little trick, like a little spring jump using my two hands to flip off the bed into the air. I took off my white G-string and dropped it on the floor. I then asked him what position he'd like. He said, "What position do you like?"

'And I said, "Well, we'll just start off in missionary then, shall we?"

'And then we did that for about four or five minutes. He was fast and furious, like he is on the pitch . . . and very strong. I pretended I was getting turned on – making the noises and going through the motions. But really I was thinking of Pot Noodles and which one to have after he'd finished: chicken and mushroom or the beef one? Wayne didn't turn me on at all – he was ugly. Then I turned over onto my knees. That went on for about two to three minutes until he finished. I knew he'd finished because the noise got a little bit more intense and he got a little more frantic. I could also see in the mirror that he just closed his eyes tight when he came.

'Afterwards, he said, "Nice one!" and thanked me very politely. Then I took the condom off, popped it in the bin and gave him some tissues, some wet ones. I started going on about his shoes as he was tying his laces. They were Prada shoes, which he said he'd had specially made. He said they were made to measure, and I said, "Oh, they're nice."

'He said he had them specially made because his feet are two different sizes and he was really proud of them.'

On pages five and six, the story was rounded off by Roo's full confession and Coleen's probable reaction to it. Unsurprisingly, the paper found that loyal friends were rallying around Wayne and Coleen in a bid to keep them together. Cynics said that she would stay with him no matter what because of the money and the deferred fame. But that didn't quite ring true. Coleen was rapidly becoming a wealthy star in her own right. Today, she has her own TV shows, magazine columns and fashion endorsements, reputedly earning £3 million a year. Even so, no girlfriend would be happy with this latest set of revelations, especially since the last embarrassment was still fresh in her mind. Remember, only a month beforehand, in December 2002, the *Sunday Mirror* had revealed that Rooney had paid 21-year-old prostitute Charlotte Glover £140 for sex. Coleen had reacted to that first exposé by storming out of the couple's luxury home in Formby, Merseyside, but days later she had decided to give Wayne another chance and move back in with him.

A friend now said, 'The most important thing for Wayne at the moment is that he keeps Coleen. He loves her more than anything else in the world and is so sorry for the hurt he has caused her. He is absolutely terrified that Coleen will walk out on him, but he's determined to make it up to her in any way he can.'

The story ran and ran – and so did the threats. Within hours, Gina

McCarrick's pimp surfaced and came on the phone demanding money with menaces and threatening extreme violence. Gina had been paid £5,000 for her story and was happy. But her pimp, who hadn't known about her deal, wanted much more and threatened to shoot me if I didn't sort him out. I had him checked out – the pimp was a drug-dealer with a reputation for violence.

A few days later, *The Sun* told that Rooney had begged for forgiveness from fiancée Coleen by offering to say sorry in front of 30,000 fans.

On the underworld front, I had more threats. The Security Boss was fuming, and a number of Evertonian gangsters had threatened to get me and anyone connected to the story.

A couple of days after our scoop, stories started to appear in other papers revealing how armed pro-Rooney vigilantes had sworn revenge on the hookers who'd kissed and told. One underworld figure was believed to have put a price on the girls' heads and they fled into hiding, in fear of their lives, begging for police protection. The story was true. Gina McCarrick had suffered repeated attack threats and abuse since doing the story.

The following week, the *Sunday Mirror* kept the story going:

> THIRTEEN celebrities, including top footballers, TV and pop stars, have been caught on video in the Rooneygate brothel scandal.
>
> They include eight Liverpool players, two from Everton, a young and handsome soap star, a major '60s rock singer and a showbiz legend. Over two years, they were all captured on CCTV as they waited to pay for sex with prostitutes including Gina McCarrick, left, at the brothel used by England and Everton superstar Wayne Rooney. In all, there are 30 security videos in a secret cache.
>
> Now this latest vice scandal threatens to become one of the most explosive ever to hit the worlds of sport and showbiz.

FOOTBALL AND GANGSTERS

The story revealed a rogues' gallery of Britain's top sports, TV and music celebrities who'd been caught on the video. To the underworld, this story was the straw that broke the camel's back. Unfortunately, Blondie was given a hard time by some ruffians and her life was made a misery – an awful consequence which I did genuinely regret. A lot of famous people had been upset – and she was paying the price.

But there was also a twist in the tale. The blackmailers and security consultants may have lost interest in Rooney after the videos were published, but a new threat was on the horizon.

Rooney had decided to quit Everton in favour of a startling move to Man United on the advice of his ambitious agent Paul Stretford. A lot of gangsters, such as The Evertonian, felt betrayed. A subsequent story revealed how Rooney and his agent had received a string of death threats from betrayed Everton bigwigs, and that Stretford had been told to stay away from Goodison.

A source revealed: 'People think this is all about Stretford cashing in and they're not happy.

'But the backlash is going to be against all of the Rooney family. Liverpool can be an unforgiving city, and there are people ready to attack the Rooneys if given the chance.'

3

Wayne Rooney: Blackmail and Extortion

Rooney's £30-million transfer from Everton to Manchester United brought with it a new phenomenon – threats from gangsters opposing the move.

Over the last few years, there have been several cases of this ugly trend. The most high-profile example occurred when Liverpool midfielder Steven Gerrard turned down an offer to go to Roman Abramovich's Chelsea after his family were intimidated by underworld figures.

In the past, good players expected fans to get upset when they left a club, especially if they went to a big rival. But today, the boos and hisses of the ordinary supporters are accompanied by a sinister undertone: death threats, hate campaigns and attacks on family members.

Several explanations can be found for this. First, the growth of the underworld in football has made gangsters confident. They try to use bully-boy tactics on players to influence decisions in the boardroom. Super-rich players may be protected by gated communities or mansions in the countryside but, at the end of the day, gangsters have a long reach and footballers are relatively easy prey.

Second, players like Wayne Rooney have been surrounded by gangsters and drug-dealers all of their lives, because of the areas they grew up in. Rooney grew up in Croxteth. The area used to be known as Smack City, because of the huge heroin epidemic which swept its estates during the Thatcher years. Drug-dealers were the new community leaders, emanating power and influence like feudal lords. The underworld elite had more of an effect on people's lives than other institutions, such as the local authorities or the police. It became ingrained in the people who lived there that if you crossed them, it was very dangerous.

Pundits have wrongly compared Rooney's upbringing to someone like George Best, equating his success to the rose-tinted rags-to-riches route followed by many footballers from poor backgrounds. Best was born into a strongly working-class community in Belfast. The area may have been poor, though, but the men had jobs in the shipyards. The province may have been ravaged by the Troubles, but traditional, working-class values were deep-rooted in the terraced streets of Best's neighbourhood.

Some parts of Rooney's neighbourhood are as far away from a traditional British working-class neighbourhood as Beverly Hills. A significant proportion of the residents of Croxteth and Norris Green form part of the new generation of underclass, where some families are third-generation unemployed. Some of the worst-element families have no values whatsoever. Although Rooney's family – especially his mother – are regarded as hard-working and responsible, some of his peers will be from homes where one or more of the parents are drug-addicts. These kids are often raised to be drug-dealers, because they know nothing else. They are out of control, carry guns and are extremely aggressive. The slightest slight can lead to shoot-outs and slayings with machetes. The gang culture is on a par with South Central Los Angeles or the slums of São Paulo. I recently spoke to a worker at a nightclub in the area where Rooney was raised. He said that the youngsters around there have stopped dancing; the lads on the magic-fuelled dance floor now stand there and shadow-box, out of their minds, in time with the aggressive beat of the drum and bass. ('Magic' is the street name for powerful, powdered Ecstasy.) That's how violent and dark the culture of what used to be Wayne's World has become.

Another explanation for the phenomenon of violent threats surrounding transfer plans is football hooliganism. Many of the old troublemakers – often the most fanatical, passionate and hot-headed fans – have grown up to be top gangsters. They still follow their teams around and, if anything hampers the team's performance, they deal with it in the only way they know how – violently.

The gangster backlash against Rooney over Man United began in late August 2004. Inexplicably, one of two gangs who were fighting a turf war against each other had threatened to target Rooney. As we'll see shortly, another celebrity, pop babe Jennifer Ellison, had already been dragged into the dispute when her family home was sprayed with machine-gun fire. So the threat was taken seriously.

I had followed this dispute for two years. One gang were drug-dealers in their early 20s who were psychotically unpredictable and armed to the teeth. The other gang were established millionaire nightclub owners. The dispute had begun when one of the young bucks had been thrown out of a nightclub for selling Ecstasy tablets. There were tit-for-tat attacks, but the war escalated when the millionaire security firm launched a call-out – a surprise raid by armed doormen – on the young bucks, which involved a machete killing in a pub. Prison sentences were handed down, and huge sums of money exchanged hands between criminals to stop further statements being made and extra jail terms ensuing.

But the war erupted once more when one of the young bucks slapped the mother of one of the security firm's powerful owners – a point of no return in underworld terms. Now, neither side was prepared to lose face. In September 2003, a car bomb exploded outside the Club 051 in the city centre.

In a suicidal show of bravado, the young bucks then began to fight back against the perceived common enemy, the police, in a bid to get them to stay out of the underworld war. That's how bad the new generation of 20-something gangsters had become. Car bombs were detonated outside two police stations – an unprecedented act of criminality. An explosion outside the police station in the Tuebrook area was the biggest on the British mainland since the IRA attacks in the 1990s.

A £50,000 bounty was placed on the head of Jennifer Ellison's fiancé Tony Richardson because of his links to the young bucks gang. In November 2003, a six-year-old girl, Makada Weaver, was shot in the chest when a gunman burst into her mother's house in the Edge Hill area of Wavertree, aiming to kill her elder brother. In a separate incident, care worker Craig Eaton was gunned down as he returned home from a night out with pals.

Then a newspaper report declared that Wayne Rooney was next on the hit list because one of the gangs wrongly linked him to a rival.

Rooney was also given 24-hour security after getting similar threats over a completely different matter. This time, they arose from his move to Manchester United, which is worth up to £30 million in the long-term, based on the player's performances. The threats were issued by ultra-fanatical fans. Detectives gave Rooney Category 1 status, meaning units would be dispatched immediately if he or his bodyguard called with a problem. Old Trafford hired an SAS-style personal minder after police told them that he and his family were targets for attacks – including one plot to petrol-bomb his car. Internet sites were filled with chilling messages from football fans against the star. Feelings were also running high amongst some gangsters who had lost money betting that Rooney would stay at Everton.

However, these various threats, though serious enough, seemed like small potatoes compared with the courtroom drama which overshadowed Rooney's final days at Everton. In football, just as in the music industry, whenever a talented new star is discovered, there is often a dispute over who spotted him earliest, who signed him up first and, most importantly, who will take a slice of his millions in wages and endorsements in the future. Most of these business battles are settled in private between scouts, agents and clubs with contractual agreements. But in Wayne Rooney's case, the greed-fuelled gold rush to get a piece of the action – to lure him away from the grass-roots agents who discovered him – led to a disagreement which immediately turned into a drama. The cast list included a convicted drug trafficker, a corrupt solicitor, the most influential football agent in the country and one of the game's playing legends. Nothing like it had ever been seen before in the beautiful game, and for the first time in the openness of a British court it showed that the underworld was well and truly entrenched amongst the back-room boys who run the sport.

Ironically, the only men who were accused of being gangsters were found to be innocent and were cleared of the blackmail charges they were facing, while the real rogues – the gangsters who had been trying to get their hands on the Wayne Rooney tapes to properly blackmail him – were left to get away scot-free. The message to the underworld was clear: 'Football is easy prey. You can carry on tightening your grip. You can carry on milking the millions unhindered.' And they have.

The story begins when Wayne Rooney was a promising 15-year-old schoolboy. He was taken under the wing of local soccer agent Peter McIntosh, a likeable and hard-working grass-roots sports executive. He had founded Pro-Form Sports Management and, in December 2000, hit on his biggest success to date, officially signing Rooney on a two-year deal.

McIntosh oversaw Rooney's transition from part-time amateur to Premiership professional at Everton. But when the big-time struck, and the boy wonder became an overnight global sensation, McIntosh claimed he was nudged out by the big boys, who swooped into town and scooped Rooney onto the books of Britain's most successful football agency, Proactive.

Proactive was the brainchild of super-agent Paul Stretford, a former vacuum-cleaner salesman from Manchester. He had started the business in a basement and watched it grow into a £20-million listed corporation. With an estimated personal wealth of about £10 million, at his height Stretford had 384 football players, managers and personalities on his books. Confidently, he set out to poach Rooney from McIntosh before his contract with Pro-Form expired in December 2002, with the help of former Liverpool and Scotland legend Kenny Dalglish. The former Footballer of the Year was a long-time friend of Stretford's, a Proactive shareholder and the company's then football operations director. Dalglish's legendary status within the game and the city of Liverpool – his dignified handling of the Hillsborough disaster had won their hearts forever – would be useful in persuading Wayne's parents to sign on the dotted line, as the 17-year-old prodigy was still too young to do so himself. Dalglish had telephoned Rooney's father, Wayne Senior, after the player's parents visited Proactive's offices in Wilmslow in May 2002 for what Stretford described as a 'credentials presentation'.

By late June that year, the Rooneys decided to plump for Proactive, and the company helped to draft a letter from them to McIntosh informing him his services would no longer be required once the current contract ran out in December 2002. For legal advice about the deal Proactive were offering, Stretford – in consultation with Dalglish and another Proactive man, former Everton youth recruitment officer Mick Doherty – pointed the Rooneys in the direction of solicitor Kevin Dooley.

Dooley, who died in June 2004 aged 62, was well known on the Liverpool football scene. His clients included Robbie Fowler, Duncan Ferguson, former Liverpool manager Roy Evans – his brother-in-law – and big names with links to Stretford, including Proactive shareholder Graeme Souness, one-time Stretford client Stan Collymore and Dalglish.

In the court case which followed, Lord Carlile QC, the barrister of John Hyland – local businessman and McIntosh's backer – told Stretford, 'You picked out, with Kenny Dalglish and Mick Doherty, the least independent solicitor you could think of.' At the time Dooley was recommended to the Rooneys, he was under investigation for a number of failed get-rich-quick schemes, which had left investors out of pocket, and for alleged corruption in the Merseyside court system. A month after Stretford wrote to him about the Rooneys, Dooley was struck off by the Law Society for dishonesty. Both Rooney's father and Stretford told the court they had been unaware of the investigations into Dooley.

McIntosh was furious, arguing that under FIFA and FA rules it was unlawful for an agent to sign-up a player while he was still under contract to another representative, i.e. him. If Stretford wanted Rooney, he would have to wait until his contract with him expired or pay him compensation. And the stakes were extremely high.

All parties knew that Rooney was the next international soccer cash cow, a new David Beckham, if not more so if abilities on the pitch translated into sporting spondoolies. Rooney may not have had Beckham's shiny branding appeal to football's new legion of aspirational, celeb-obsessed fans, but Rooney connected to the game's gritty grass roots, from Stockport and Streatham to the satellited-up shanty towns of Sri Lanka and Shanghai, a scally who pirouetted around players like a Russian ballerina dancing around icicles, a goal attacker with the aggression of a 17-year-old American Marine in Baghdad, a footballing genius with a lightning-quick mind, in terms of play-making vision, as big as Gordon Brown's, a street kid who had the hunger for success of a Cuban refugee drug-dealer who had just landed in Miami. The World was Wayne's. And no one was arguing. No one knew where it was going exactly, but everyone knew it was going to end up in a big pile of dough at some stage.

Forgetting all of the back-page puns and hypery, it was one small but vital quality that made Rooney stand out. He played as if he had no respect. On the pitch, like so many other rookie players, he didn't seem to care for reputations. Put him up against David Beckham, Ronaldo, Rio Ferdinand, Ronaldinho – Rooney did not care for their reputations. He went into his tackles arrogantly. He was a child of the hoodie generation.

As the suits squared up to each other, the predictions came true. By the time of his 19th birthday, a £30-million move to Manchester United had made Rooney a rich man already. His wages went up to £3 million a year, while his profile as England's key player for the next decade meant income from his image rights could be expected to generate tens of millions more. Stretford took a £1.5-million commission on the Man United move.

FOOTBALL AND GANGSTERS

McIntosh and his business partners, Dave Lockwood and John Hyland, tried to bring Stretford to the table to claim a share of the riches they saw slipping from their grasp. Initially, the talks went well. Stretford, 46, signed Rooney on a two-year football contract in September 2002. 'We decided Wayne would be better off in their [Proactive's] hands. They seemed more professional,' said Wayne Senior. But by November 2002, when it became an open secret that Rooney was on his way to Proactive, the talks stalled when Stretford refused Hyland's request for a lump-sum compensation payment and a percentage of Rooney's future revenue.

The dispute then suddenly took a sinister turn. One day, Dalglish asked Stretford how the Rooney saga was going, and he replied, 'Not very well.' Dalglish offered to set up a meeting, which Hyland attended, at Heathrow Airport. Stretford said later that on his arrival he was taken by Dalglish and another man to the Le Meridien Hotel, where, waiting in the lobby, was Tommy Adams, a notorious gangster who ruled north London and far beyond. Adams had been released six months earlier from a seven-and-a-half-year sentence for cannabis trafficking. Stretford denied bringing in 'the heavy mob' or knowing whether Dalglish had helped to arrange Adams's presence. Stretford told police that Adams was there 'to arbitrate'.

A week after the Heathrow encounter, Stretford met Hyland at the Moss Nook restaurant, near Manchester Airport, with a bag containing £250,000 in cash. Stretford was apparently going to bung Hyland the money as a settlement, a pay-off to make him go away. William Lindfield, a security consultant hired by Stretford, later told police he sat in a Mercedes guarding the cash while Hyland and Stretford were in a discussion. It was a futile gesture. There was no way that businessman Hyland was going to get involved in grubby cash payments.

In February 2003, Stretford, Jeanette Rooney and her son became the only directors of Stoneygate 48 Ltd. Wayne Junior owns the two £1 shares in a business which exists to exploit his image rights. Stretford's company, which made £1.5 million out of Rooney's move to United, holds an eight-year licence to manage those rights and take its cut.

Fractious negotiations continued into the next year, and, on 2 May 2003, Stretford received an email from Lockwood, who was taking care of day-to-day negotiations with Stretford at this point, proposing a settlement. Proactive would pay around half the profits from Rooney for ten years to a company called IMRA Management Consultants Ltd. The company is registered at the Manchester offices of Lockwood's lawyers, Nexus Solicitors. However, for many different reasons, the deal never went through.

In March, three gunshots were fired at Stretford's next-door neighbour's house in Wilmslow, Cheshire. They were blasted at the neighbour's front door, but Stretford feared the shots were meant for him. His £1-million luxury house is just 100 yards from the home of Sir Alex Ferguson, boss of Manchester United. However, it was a false alarm. It was later proved that the incident was totally unrelated to the Rooney dispute or Stretford.

The next meeting took place at a hotel near Warrington on the evening of 4 June 2003, the day after Rooney, then 17 and Everton's greatest asset, had won his fourth England cap. Stretford had arranged to meet Dave Lockwood, owner of the X8 agency which had purchased a stake in McIntosh's company, Pro-Form Sports Management. Half an hour into their meeting, they were joined, apparently unexpectedly, by Hyland, a 42-year-old former butcher and boxer turned promoter, and two men Stretford did not know, the Bacon brothers. The meeting then acquired a sinister edge, Stretford would later claim. Stretford found himself surrounded. To his left, Hyland thumped the table where Stretford sat as he shouted at the agent and demanded the 'scheming little prick' sign away 50 per cent of the profits from Rooney for the next ten years, which was the deal Stretford had allegedly agreed to earlier. Sources close to Hyland dismissed Stretford's attempts to paint the meeting as sinister and intimidating. A source said, 'This tough talk is no different from what goes on in boardrooms up and down the land. It's got to be seen in context. Stretford had messed Hyland around for a long time and tempers were fraying.'

FOOTBALL AND GANGSTERS

As Hyland was telling him off, Anthony Bacon, a security consultant and former member of the Australian SAS, looked on from the right. His younger brother, Christopher, skilled in judo, boxing and no-holds-barred ultimate fighting, bent close to Stretford's face and said, chillingly, 'If you want to play the gangster bit, bring any man you want into it. Doesn't mind me, it's one of those . . . honestly, that's my game. Do you understand that?'

'Yeah,' replied Stretford.

When Hyland and the Bacon brothers left, Lockwood expressed astonishment. 'Got a f***ing candid camera?' he asked.

'No,' replied Stretford. In fact, he had had the entire exchange captured on a hidden camera and a microphone secreted in a coffee machine. Later, Stretford claimed that the ordeal was 'as close as I've ever come to someone saying, "Right, I'm going to take you out."' Other sources said he was overplaying the problem, which, at the end of the day, was self-made.

Stretford was so concerned that he decided to tell Wayne himself and his parents for the first time about the dispute. On 11 June 2003, just hours before Rooney was to play an England international against Slovakia – his fifth-ever cap – Stretford held a meeting with the family. He claimed that he was being blackmailed and intimidated by gangsters, who wanted a cut of Rooney's fortune. Later, the implication was that Rooney's head was wrecked by the nightmare news, destroying his form during the game. He was substituted at half-time, before England limped home to a 2–1 victory.

The millionaire agent then stated that he was going to front it out by employing minders. Wayne Senior and Jeanette knocked back his offer of bodyguards, instead opting to boost security on their new £400,000 home in the Sandfield Park area of Liverpool, partly owned by Everton Football Club.

At the beginning of July, security was upgraded at the Rooneys' house. State-of-the-art CCTV was installed to warn of any intruders in the grounds, with two cameras clearly visible in a tree at the front of the house. A steel plate was also fixed against the bars of the cast-iron gates to the sweeping driveway. To put distance between himself and these worries, Wayne also spent £30,000 taking his family and girlfriend on a holiday in Mexico.

News of the ongoing dispute began to leak out. About a week later, on 6 July 2003, the *News of the World* scooped Fleet Street and ran a story stating that Stretford and Rooney were being blackmailed. Though the story clearly referred to the background Hyland dispute, it didn't name Hyland or give details of the dispute – mainly because it was completely untrue that he was blackmailing Stretford. The gun attack on Stretford's neighbour that the paper reported had frightened the agent was later proved to be unrelated to him. However, despite the mix-ups, the story contained some fascinating information about the drama. The front-page headline was 'ROONEY MURDER PLOT: Gangsters threaten to cripple star and kill agent'.

> SOCCER wonderkid Wayne Rooney is at the centre of a terrifying murder threat. Confronted by reporters, Stretford said, 'This is a very dangerous situation and I'm now going to have to consult with a lot of people. It's dangerous for me and my family. I'm not prepared to say another word on this issue.'

A *News of the World* journalist later told me that the paper had been given the story by a long-standing tipster, whom we'll call Jay-Jay Calf (not his real name). Calf was a former heroin-dealer turned celebrity bodyguard who had sold the paper a story a few years earlier about a very famous comedian who liked going to see prostitutes. In more recent years, he had tried to get hired by former Liverpool striker Robbie Fowler by warning off intrusive reporters without the footy star's knowledge and ingratiating himself with Fowler's then lawyer Kevin Dooley (whom we have aleady met), who was later exposed for corruption.

However, some cynical media observers claimed that sources close to

FOOTBALL AND GANGSTERS

Stretford had planted the story in a skilful PR ploy to make the threats public to scare off the alleged blackmailers and so to reduce further risk to Stretford. The *News of the World* suggested that the threats came from two notorious crime families in London and Liverpool who had made their first demands in December. Stretford was even apparently threatened by the gangsters personally when they turned up in his office. In the article, a source close to Stretford went into more detail:

> Paul is absolutely terrified about the threat to him and his family. He took the problem to several heavy-duty close-protection agencies, seeking their advice and round-the-clock protection. It was clear that those at the centre of this were very frightened and that they felt genuine fear for their safety. They understood there was a death threat to Stretford and that if he did not do what was wanted, Rooney would also be drawn in – that he could be targeted too. It was mentioned that his legs could be broken. When the protection agencies heard the names of the gangsters involved and checked into their background, they decided this was not a job they fancied. There were guns involved and some very bad blood. Most of the agencies just decided they did not want to be involved at all, and they backed straight off. They did not want to know; it was just too hot to handle. It was clear that this was not just some bunch of petty criminals putting on the clamps here. We are talking about men who feel they have a grievance and are prepared to use guns to put it right. Stretford clearly knew all this and was rightly worried. As a result, he has spent a lot of time abroad recently to avoid this conflict. But he is fed up of running away from the problem. The truth is that football is built on competition, and certain people are jealous of his success. They want a slice of the action. Stretford is a supreme operator and a great professional, and it seems some people are deeply envious.

The sensational story was followed up in the dailies. The *Daily Star* revealed that rival gangsters had stepped in to defend Rooney, led by his old protector The Evertonian. Under the headline 'LAY FINGER ON ROONEY AND YOU'RE DEAD MEAT', the story revealed how gangsters threatening Rooney had been warned off – by other gangsters. The mobster said:

> Nobody is going to harm him while I'm around – nothing will happen to him. I support Everton myself and if something happened to Wayne then I'd lay bets Liverpool would kick off again.
>
> It would be like a war. Even though he doesn't know it, Wayne has got a lot of friends who'll stick up for him.

Interestingly, the article revealed that the threats had been officially denied by the police, even after meetings between club officials and the Cheshire constabulary.

But, two months later, the picture changed. Following a formal complaint from Stretford, police arrested Hyland, and Chris and Anthony Bacon, for blackmail, based on the secret videotapes of the tub-thumping Warrington meeting. A police source said, 'The arrests are the result of a lengthy investigation which has involved Mr Stretford working closely with police.' However, from the outset, bemused Hyland totally denied the charges.

Two years later, in October 2004, the trial kicked off. Almost immediately, cracks began to appear in the prosecution case that gave glimpses of a murky situation in which gangsters were clearly involved but the men in the dock were definitely not.

The jury was surprised to be told that squeaky-clean Dalglish had invited Tommy Adams to a meeting.

'The stakes were enormous,' a jury was told.

Stretford claimed in evidence that he felt intimidated at seeing a 'London villain' present and the meeting became heated when Hyland

and the others could not get Stretford to sign a deal on their terms. Dalglish and Adams apparently said little but Dalglish, a former Footballer of the Year, then refused to give a police statement.

In court, Stretford said he felt let down by Dalglish. 'I have had a great and long relationship with Kenny Dalglish, and yes, I felt let down by him.'

Stretford himself was accused of wanting Adams present. 'You knew full well that Kenny Dalglish had engineered for Tommy Adams to come and facilitate this meeting,' Lord Carlile, Hyland's barrister, said in court. 'It was you who brought the heavy mob, wasn't it?'

Stretford denied this and said it was 'fear and confusion' that prevented him from leaving the meeting.

Rooney's move to United had been precipitated by apparent interest from Newcastle United, who, despite the presence at the club already of four top-class strikers, including former England captain Alan Shearer, tabled a £20-million transfer bid.

In court, Lord Carlile asked Stretford about this, wondering if the bid was genuine or a ruse to inflate Rooney's eventual price and draw Manchester United into an early deal. 'I don't think anyone makes a bid of £20 million to another club if they don't mean it,' said Stretford. 'We were very prepared for the Newcastle bid to be accepted and for Wayne to negotiate with Newcastle United.'

Others, again, beg to differ. 'Rooney was never going to sign for Newcastle,' says the agent who spoke to *The Observer*. 'I think Freddy Shepherd [Newcastle's chairman] was used by Stretford. He won't think he's been used, but that is what has happened.'

During legal arguments – the jury had not yet been sworn in – the judge heard of Stretford's 'cash bung'. Moreover, it seemed as though the prosecution had not disclosed to the defence the evidence of a security consultant, William Lindfield. Hyland's barrister, Lord Carlile QC, said Lindfield worked for Mr Stretford and drove him to a meeting with Hyland at a Manchester restaurant in 2002. Lord Carlile said, 'It is part of our case that Mr Stretford offered John Hyland cash.'

Stretford broke down in tears during the case and said he had developed an 'arthritic nature in my foot caused by the stress'.

The final nail in the coffin for Stretford was just around the corner. Astonishingly, he was exposed in court for not telling the whole truth under oath.

In his evidence, Stretford had claimed he did not poach Rooney from McIntosh while he was still under contract. But two documents came to light during a weekend break in the proceedings that showed that Stretford had reached an agreement with the England striker by September 2002, three months before his contract with McIntosh expired.

Prosecutor John Hedgecoe told Warrington Crown Court, 'Having seen these documents, we do not feel able to rely on Paul Stretford as a witness in this case. And in view of his importance as a witness, we offer no further evidence.'

Hyland and the Bacon brothers immediately walked free, and after the case Hyland called for a review of the way football agents operate. It was a great victory for the three men.

His lawyer Peter Quinn said, 'The FA and Premier League should appoint an independent person to start an inquiry in public as soon as possible.' In the aftermath of the collapsed trial, McIntosh and Hyland are pursuing a civil case against Stretford and Proactive, now part of the Formation Group, for compensation on losing out on Rooney. There has been a series of court hearings to decide preliminary legal arguments, mainly in connection with fees and costs, and the case is proceeding. Stretford resigned as a Formation director but remains head of player representation and Formation's largest shareholder, with a 12 per cent shareholding.

When Rooney made his debut for Manchester United on 28 September 2004 – scoring a hat-trick against Fenerbahce SK in the Champions League at Old Trafford – his £30-million fee seemed instantly justified. The risk of signing Rooney for such a high price had paid off for the United manager, Sir Alex Ferguson, and the club's chief executive, David Gill. But beyond the razzmatazz of the transfer, the Hyland–Stretford court case seemed to bring the whole show back down to earth, highlighting just how badly football needed regulating.

4

Steven Gerrard: Taxmen and Drug-Dealer

Cool-headed England midfielder Steven Gerrard was terrorised for four years by a crazed drug-dealer over his love affair with a teenage model.

Gerrard was threatened with death and put under round-the-clock protection by armed police officers. George Bromley Junior threatened to shoot the Liverpool hero on sight, threw a brick through the window of his £50,000 BMW and pursued him through the streets in a high-speed car chase. The mental torture of being trapped in an underworld feud led to an infamous dip in form for Gerrard.

In a separate case, another set of thugs were planning to extort and blackmail Gerrard for a slice of his then £60,000-a-week wages in one of the first cases of systematic 'taxing' in football.

Taxing is when gangsters force people to hand over money by threatening to do harm to them. The process is age old, but in recent years specialised gangs have begun to target footballers specifically, mainly because of their high wages and vulnerability. Many football stars are young and inexperienced and fail to manage confrontation effectively. Their glitzy lifestyles, often involving more women and booze than is good for them, also leave them open to abuse. The risk of appearing centre-stage in a press scandal is another chink in their armour that the underworld has been quick to home in on.

Many players have been brought up in tough neighbourhoods where gangsterism is ingrained – and all too many fail to distance themselves from the hangers-on who pose as mates. Footballers have a habit of socialising in places where the wrong people hang out: often in city-centre nightclubs and hotels where the gangsters love to do their business.

All of these factors add up to easy prey for villains, leading to an increase in taxing – the unspeakable crime that is plaguing British football.

I broke the world-exclusive story about Gerrard's trouble with gangsters in 2003. The first tip I received involved the blackmail plot, centring around two members of a north Liverpool crime family known as The Taxmen. The Taxmen had successfully blackmailed a string of soccer stars, including a former Everton player whose tragic case will be dealt with later in the book.

They now turned their attention to the new kid on the block: Gerrard. Their modus operandi was crude but effective. The plan had worked like a treat in previous cases.

Stage One: the Honeytrap

First, they would groom a young, pretty female to infiltrate the footballer's inner circle of friends. Or, failing that, they would try to get one of the existing female hangers-on onside and on board for a future conspiracy.

Stage Two: the Scandal

They would instruct their honeytrap spy to manipulate a scandal or, failing that, fabricate an incident such as sexual assault or rape. This would preferably involve the main target, the player, but the scam worked equally well with one of his close friends or family. For instance, the girl might say she was drugged and assaulted by one of the player's pals – but the sting in the tail is that the phoney incident took place at a party at the soccer star's house or during a night out with the player and his entourage or in the hotel where he was staying. Therefore, the scandal is subtly but irrefutably linked to the player. Like all good cons, the plan is based on clever psychology; in this case, the nub is guilt by association. Even if he was not responsible, the player would know that he was most vulnerable because, as the most high-profile member of the group, he had the most to lose. He was the one who would be scandalised – just like in the Chappaquiddick scandal involving Ted Kennedy.

Stage Three: the Friendly Offer

The gangsters would then appoint a non-gang member to front the final stages of the scam, a friendly middleman to liaise between the gangsters and the soccer star's camp. Like an assassin, he would come with a smiling face. He was probably a friend or an associate that the star had known all his life. The middleman would approach the soccer star and state that there was a girl going around town claiming that she had been assaulted by the footballer or one of his pals. But luckily, the middleman would say, the girl was related to a well-known gangster family. She was 'one of theirs'. A lie would be told that the honeytrap was one of the daughters or sister of a well-known gangster.

The middleman would then state that the girl had been traumatised by the incident and had been on her way to the police station to report the attack when she was persuaded, as laid down by the underworld code, to leave the police out of it and sort it out under the table, between the two parties. So the middleman would present himself as someone who had done the player a favour and would help to solve the problem – a classic protection-racket tactic.

Stage Four: the Carrot and Sting

The middleman would then say that the best way to sort it out was to pay the girl to go away – give her some unofficial compensation to forget all about it so that everyone would be happy. 'It doesn't matter if it's true or not, or who did what, or who says this or that. The easiest thing to do is pay the slag off and get the whole thing binned forever.' Something like that would be said to persuade the footballer to pay up. She'd get over it and the papers would never need to find out. The middleman would then load the friendly offer of help with an undertone of threat to help move the deal along more quickly. 'Obviously, the gangsters are very pissed off that you've been taking liberties with their girls. But they know what it's like with young lads and booze and all the rest of it. And, at the end of the day, they're big fans of the club. They understand that it wasn't you or you wouldn't normally behave like this so they're going to give you a walkover. If you pay the girl, then it will all be forgotten about.'

The player now has three options. First, go to the police. The law will investigate the blackmail allegations, but these claims will be hard to prove bearing in mind the subtlety and sneakiness of the friendly offer. Plus, there is a risk they will also investigate the sexual-assault allegations. Players often feel they will be dragged into a your-word-against-hers situation, like so many young footballers have been in the rape and roasting scandals in the last few years. Either way, no matter what, you're going in the papers. Once an official complaint is logged, it only takes one call from a journalist to a police press office to stand up a story.

The second option is to fight fire with fire: to contract a rival gang of villains to lean on the villains who are leaning on you. This is extremely dangerous, unpredictable and costly. One Premiership player paid £30,000 to gangsters to protect him from a psychopathic extortionist, expecting that they would have a menacing word with the attacker. Without his consent, his new protectors kidnapped the extortionist and shot him – not fatally, but the extreme behaviour frightened the player. Another player became embroiled in a dispute over a girlfriend. Some heavies took it upon themselves to help the beleagured player, leading to an unforeseen escalation in the conflict. The feud ended only after the player was beaten, stabbed and forced to leave the high-profile club he worshipped. Despite being known as one of the game's hard-men, he never fully recovered from his underworld ordeal. His career went into decline, his marriage fell apart and he became addicted to drink and drugs before fleeing Britain altogether.

Standing up to the gangsters has occasionally worked. In one case, a very talented international player was being taxed £10,000 every time he went on a night out with his pals. The player had become embroiled in a feud with a nightclub security firm after he insulted a female guest at a popular nightspot. Once again, this was a pretext – part of a honeytrap tax sting. He told the girl that she was a slag. Bad move. The girl was connected to the underworld. The player had been drunk and abusive and completely out of order, but he was not prepared for what was to come. He was repeatedly attacked and threatened and told that every time he was seen out on the town he would have to pay £10,000. Once, after an away game in Leeds, he was invited by a pop-group singer to go for a drink when they returned to their home city. He confessed the problem and explained that he was scared to death. Time passed, and the problem refused to go away, until word of it eventually reached a security firm in Ireland with connections to the IRA. The paramilitary-backed gangsters seemingly had a word with the villains on his case. The problem quickly disappeared.

The major downside to the fight-back option is the considerable risk of the tactic backfiring – of the villains you have turned to for help turning around after frightening off the aggressors and saying, 'Now that we have got your enemies off your case, we would like paying every month for further protection.' So, in effect, the player has replaced one set of taxmen with another.

The third option for a player caught in the crossfire is the pay-off – to go along with the gangsters' demands. Unfortunately, for many victims new to the underworld, they opt for this path of least resistance. It offers them a workable solution to a nerve-wracking predicament.

Meanwhile, England and Liverpool midfielder Steven Gerrard was about to be the next target of the Taxmen gang. Armed with their tried and tested battle plan, The Taxmen began making preparations and gathering intelligence. But they quickly discovered that squeaky-clean Gerrard did not get himself into compromising situations. Though he was young, free and single (this was before he met his long-term partner Alex Curran), as well as obscenely cash-rich, Gerrard lived a low-key existence. He did not womanise or hell-raise. But he did have pals who were vulnerable, and The Taxmen soon discovered that Gerrard and his mates often went out drinking in the bars and clubs of Southport seaside resort, near his luxury crash pad. Sometimes, they would go back to Gerrard's house to relax with a nightcap.

The Taxmen then recruited a honeytrap to infiltrate Gerrard's entourage. She was told to hang around the same nightspots as Gerrard and to lure one of his mates into a compromising situation. The honeytrap was instructed in detail. First, she would engineer herself an invite back to Gerrard's flat. She would pretend to be drunk and then force herself onto one of Gerrard's pals. In the early hours of the morning, she would leave without a fuss. The next day, she would complain that she had been sexually assaulted. She would not go to the police but raise it with a friend to act as a potential witness. She would not say she'd had sex with the pal. She'd say that, while she was intoxicated, the pal masturbated over her. If she said she'd had full sex, some physical evidence of it would be sought. But instead she would say that, like many victims of sex attacks, she'd cleaned up as soon as she'd got home.

The plan was put into action and the honeytrap girl secretly shadowed Gerrard and his group for several weeks. But despite her best efforts, and no matter how revealingly she dressed or available she made herself, Gerrard and his pals did not fall for her charms. The operation dragged on until details began to leak out to the wider underworld. Another well-known Liverpool crime family got wind of the plot. As well as being fanatical Liverpool fans, members of the crime clan personally knew members of Gerrard's Huyton-based family. They felt some loyalty towards him and decided to act unilaterally. A meeting was called between the two gangs and The Taxmen were warned gently to stay clear of Gerrard. Combined with the fact that the plans didn't seem to be working anyway, The Taxmen decided to leave him well alone.

However, to make doubly sure that The Taxmen did not go back on their word, the story was leaked to me, presumably in the hope that the threat of public exposure would force the gang to abandon their plans. The fans in Liverpool are extremely protective of their players, especially their home-grown heroes, and The Taxmen knew a public outcry would be very, very bad for them. They would lose support on the streets – vital for any organised-crime unit – and other villains would gang up on them.

I travelled to Liverpool to investigate in the hope of standing the story up. It was a long shot, because the only people who knew the facts were The Taxmen themselves, and they were unlikely to talk. I got the address of the main man and drove around to knock on his door. As always, I checked with an underworld contact to find out the likely response of the Mr Big to an approach by Her Majesty's press. 'He'll knock you out on his doorstep,' I was told. 'He's a dog. In fact, you won't even get as far as the door, because his house is camera'd-up to death. They see you coming in and cop for you on the path. Bad idea.'

As I didn't fancy being made to lie down and go to sleep at the hands of a muscle-bound, stead-head villain, I opted for plan B. Often, the best way of getting to a 'community leader' is going through another well-known community leader, preferably a bigger one. First of all, I phoned the boss of a door-security company in the north-west. Mr Doorteam often had the inside track on football and gangsters because the players kept coming to his clubs. He told me that he knew all about the taxing of Gerrard, but he couldn't give any more help because of the delicate underworld politics involved. Plus, he was knee-deep in a very violent gangwar of his own, in which many men had been stabbed, shot, burned and even blown up with explosives.

One of the most powerful godfathers in the city owed me a favour, so I went to him at the hotel he used as his personal fiefdom. The godfather phoned up the main taxman and said, 'I've got a reporter here who's asked me to give you a ring. There's a story going round that

Steven Gerrard was gonna get taxed and he wondered whether you knew anything about it.'

The godfather was an expert in dealing with prickly situations, very diplomatic and very worldly wise. He continued, 'He doesn't mean any disrespect by it. In fact, he come to me out of respect to both you and myself. He just wanted to mark your card.'

Of course, the taxman denied any involvement. There was no way he was ever going to admit it, even to a fellow underworld legend, but it was worth a try. However, a new lead suddenly cropped up: I got the name of the honeytrap girl. Unfortunately, she turned out to be a 21-year-old niece of the taxman, so I knew he would tip her off that the papers were on the case and that she should keep her mouth shut. I got her address, a new-style semi-detached house in the Kirkdale area of Liverpool.

I went there at about 3.00 p.m. She was still in bed, but she came to the door as cool as a salad and said, 'I don't know anything about it.' And that was that – door closed and straight back to her pot-fumed pit. I rang the bell a few times, but I knew from experience that it was foolish to push it on a doorstep like this. It would only end up in the boot of a car.

After hitting this dead end, I went back to London. But the following day, important news arrived from the front. I got a call from Mr Doorteam. He said that he had some info on the Gerrard story for me. So I turned around and headed up to Liverpool again on the first train out. I arranged to meet him outside Lime Street Station that evening at 11.30 – the arrival time of the last train from Euston. He insisted I come alone.

It was a cold, January night and the concourse was windswept and deserted. My mobile went off. Mr Doorteam told me to move out of the station and stand near the main road in front of the historic St George's Hall. I was clearly under surveillance. Mr Doorteam was making sure that I was not trying to turn him over. He was checking that I wasn't accompanied by any unwanted colleagues, particularly long-lens photographers who were going to snap him. After about five minutes in the open, where they could see I was alone, I was told to walk towards the Empire theatre and wait near the postbox outside. My first thought was that I was going to get shot or put in the boot of a fast-moving snatch vehicle. But it was too late to back out now.

Within seconds, a black Hackney cab had pulled up next to the phonebox. 'Are you Graham?' barked the driver.

'Yes.'

'Jump in the back, quick.'

I got in and the taxi sped off. Suddenly, I got a very frightening shock. There was a man sat on the floor with his back to one of the spring-loaded seats attached to the driver partition. He was dressed in dark clothing. He was wearing a huge, black Schott snorkel parka with the hood zipped right to the end to form a long cylinder of fur-rimmed material so I couldn't see his face. There was just a dark space where his face should have been. I guess that's why they call them snorkel parkas, because they do zip up into a proper snorkel so that you can breathe. He reminded me of one of those schoolkids in the '70s who kept getting knocked over because they couldn't look right or left in the parkas – like the little brother in the film *East is East* who never took his snorkel off, but much more sinister.

No one said anything until we were well off the plot. I thought that it was the end, that I was trapped in a black cab – doors locked, by the way (I'd spied the little red light flick on immediately) – with a man trying to conceal his identity. However, the man soon identified himself. It was Mr Doorteam himself, whom I'd only ever spoken to on the phone.

He explained that he'd feared I would try to snatch (secretly photograph) him. The first thing he did was take a picture of me using a mobile phone. 'I've got something for you. But if you ever say where you got it from, then I've got your picture and I'll find you.'

Next, he instructed the driver to park up and he gave me two pieces of paper. The documents were part of a Merseyside Police intelligence file on Steven Gerrard. They explained how Gerrard's life was under threat from a local drug-dealer.

I quickly scanned it under the weak ceiling lights in the cab, memorising every detail. Meanwhile, I was keeping an eye on everything that was going on around me, as well as trying to figure out the bigger picture.

Why was Mr Doorteam doing this? Why was he handing me an award-winning story on a plate? Certainly not for the cash – he lived in a mansion outside of Liverpool, drove an underworld-standard four-by-four such as a Porsche Cayenne or a Lexus Jeep, and earned a fortune.

Then I got on to it. This was part peace offering, part diversionary tactic but mostly part PR sweetener. Often, when a celebrity is in deep trouble with a newspaper, his PR people will offer the reporters an alternative, more anodyne story to keep the scandalous one from going public. And the gangsters were using the same tactic.

The message was loud and clear: 'This is a better story than the taxman story. You're never going to stand the taxman story up anyway, so you may as well get stuck in to this much juicier one and leave the taxman alone. We're telling you to get off the taxman's case in a very nice way.' Nothing was said explicitly, but that was the game. As I've said, gangsters today are as media-savvy as PR people in showbiz and sport. Obviously, after I had phoned Mr Doorteam the day before, he had phoned the taxman and they had hatched the spoiler plan together. Enter the murky world of football and gangsters, where the deal is king.

I gave the document back but memorised the key names. Obviously, I would not play their game, but at the same time I would not let this story slip. If I had the names of the cast list, I could do the story myself. I did not get a copy of the 'threat assessment' at that point, but I later got a copy of a similar document.

A threat assessment is an official police intelligence document which does what it says on the tin: the report tries to gauge whether a particular threat is serious and to identify the risks facing the subject – in this case Steven Gerrard – by pulling in all available information from official files, informants and police meetings. The documents often conclude by recommending what type of action the police should take to reduce the risks. This one directed officers to monitor the movements of the potential assailant, Bromley Junior, and to warn Gerrard of the threat and advise him to beef up his security.

I asked Mr Doorteam where he got the intelligence document from, to confirm authenticity. He said that a publican had got it off a bent copper. I suspected that this was a lie. Though the paperwork may have originated through an unauthorised leak, it was more likely that they'd got it from other villains in an attempt to win a security contract from Gerrard to fend off the threat. Either way, I was 99 per cent sure it was genuine.

The nub of the story was simple: drug-dealer George Bromley Junior was threatening to shoot Gerrard because they were both chasing the same girl, shopgirl Lauren Ashcroft.

To stand the story up, I needed to get chats with Ashcroft and Bromley. I knew that Gerrard, Merseyside Police and the FA were unlikely to talk, but if I got other witnesses, even a couple, I wouldn't need them.

Lauren Ashcroft was a pretty, teenage Scouse girl who worked in a sports shop in a grim Liverpool shopping centre. She had long-since stopped going out with Gerrard and Bromley, and was quietly getting on with her life. I found out where she lived and went round there. Both Lauren and her mum seemed very down to earth, and initially they were very wary about talking to a reporter. Her dad, a former doorman and fanatical Liverpool fan, was in prison at the time on a gun and Ecstasy-tablet racket, which was fortunate for me. No doubt, he would have tried to flatten me if he'd opened the door and I'd started asking questions about footballers and gangsters – and his lovely daughter. In my years of crunching gravel and banging on doors in pursuit of stories, I had learned that doormen like to knock people out – especially reporters – and answer questions later. I have been chased by men wielding batons and, in one case, pursued back to my hotel and held hostage for 24 hours.

In the event, Lauren and her mum told me enough. I was amazed at how young and petite Lauren seemed – fragile almost – for someone who was at the centre of a violent situation. There was no doubt she was good looking – she had aspirations to be a model – but her manner was ordinary and she had the mousey, unconfident ways of a schoolgirl who had not yet come out of her shell.

Lauren told me that she had met Gerrard two years earlier, when she was 15. Gerrard was 20 at the time and making a big name for himself at Liverpool. The young couple had a very innocent courtship, a typically modern popcorn and multi-screen love affair. But, three months later, the couple were forced to break up because of Gerrard's footy commitments. The split was amicable and they remained pals, Gerrard occasionally popping around to her house, as much to see Lauren's Liverpool-mad dad, Peter, as anything.

By this time, Lauren had started dating Liverpool's answer to Tony 'Scarface' Montana, a rootin'-tootin', shoot-'em-up drug-dealer called George Bromley Junior. Bromley was already infamous because of his family name. His father, George Bromley Senior, had been a notorious extortionist who forced drug-dealers to pay him tax under threat of extreme torture. His terrible trademark was to steam-iron the testicles of his victims to force them into giving up their drug-dealing profits. His MO was simple. He would often burst into a drug-dealer's house, strip him and tie him up in front of his wife and kids. Then he would turn to the wife and say, 'Is there an iron in the house, love?' It was a good choice of torture weapon; every house has got one and you don't have to carry one to and from jobs. After plugging it in, Bromley Senior would warn his terrified prey: 'You've got until the iron warms up to tell me where you keep the cash.'

Like father, like son; George Bromley Junior was psychopathically violent. He saw red when flashy Gerrard turned up at his girlfriend's family home – and subjected the star to a series of attacks. Gerrard was now caught up in a deadly love triangle, whether he liked it or not. The terror campaign affected him badly, and his game went to pot for a while as he struggled to get it sorted.

First of all, around January 2001, Gerrard received straightforward, no-nonsense death threats from the gangster, who left him in no doubt that his fury was a direct result of the player's continued connection with the teenage model. As a result, armed police were quickly drafted in to protect him. The threats went some way towards explaining Gerrard's dramatic loss of form during that season. At one point, he was banned for three games at an FA disciplinary hearing for a violent tackle. The cause of Gerrard's dip in form was cryptically referred to by Liverpool manager Gerard Houllier in November 2002. After hauling him off the pitch during a vital European match against Basle in Switzerland, Houllier fumed, 'The problem is not physical with Stevie; maybe it's a matter of his environment. I'm frustrated in him.' And he was not wrong. Gerrard continued to be subjected to a series of frightening incidents, including being chased in his car through the streets of Liverpool. During one exchange, Gerrard was challenged to a bare-knuckle fight by a furious Bromley.

Police implemented a thorough review of his security and ordered Football Association chiefs to step up security around the player while he was on England duty. A threat analysis was drawn up and his luxury home in Southport and family home in Liverpool were studied. Police armed-response vehicles were instructed to patrol outside his apartment in Southport and a 24-hour watch was also put on his mother's house in Huyton, Liverpool. A police source said: 'It was feared Bromley had access to firearms, and he was shadowed continually by officers for weeks. He was not only warned to stay away from Gerrard, but the police were constantly on his case. They never gave him a minute's peace. He was always being pulled up for the slightest offences, even for not wearing a seat belt. This was a police tactic to let him know that we were watching him in case he made a move on Gerrard.'

In November 2001, a gang of hoodlums threw a brick at the window of Gerrard's luxury silver BMW X5 when it was parked outside Lauren's home near Anfield stadium. Lauren said, 'Steven was sitting there and I went next door to get a cup of sugar. Then Steven told me, "They've thrown a brick at my car." He was on the couch looking out. He didn't see who it was. I was shocked.' The car was scratched and dented. Lauren made a statement to the police and told them that she wasn't sure who had attacked the car, though her friends claimed that her angry boyfriend Bromley was behind it. Lauren was dating Bromley full-time now. They remained a couple for nine months after her relationship with Gerrard had finished, but they eventually fell out and split up. A friend of Lauren's added, 'Her parents were not happy with her seeing Bromley. He was pretty flash, with nice cars and plenty of money. But when she finished with him, he would not let her go, even though he had other girlfriends. He was trying to get her back. He was a jealous boyfriend, and was not a nice person.'

Gerrard fell for Lauren when she was still at school. But she was working part-time in a sunbed salon and Gerrard would pop in for a cup of tea and a chat. He was just 20 and had burst into the Liverpool first team and already was being touted as one of England's brightest stars. Lauren said, 'We met by accident. I was with one of his close mates, Jonathan Boggan, and Steven kept staring at me. Jonathan introduced us and he gave him my mobile number. He kept phoning and asking me out, but I didn't know who he was. I didn't know anything about football. He was a very normal person. He's very friendly and down to earth.'

A friend of the family said, 'Sometimes, they'd go to the pictures or go out for nice meals or just stay in. She said he was very fit and nice looking. She was still at school and didn't tell her friends, but word did get out. She wouldn't let him pick her up from school, because she felt it would be showing off. He was her first serious boyfriend, though. But she did not have a clue about football. She started keeping a scrapbook of cuttings when articles and pictures of him appeared in the papers. She'd only ever been to a match once before, when she was about ten with her dad, so she didn't know anything about the game. Steven once gave her £100 to go out one night when he couldn't make it. But Lauren didn't want his money, so she gave it back to her mum so she could return it to him.'

Gerrard used to stay over at her family home after a match but always in separate rooms, sleeping in his girlfriend's younger brother's bed.

He innocently became friends with Lauren's dad, Peter Ashcroft, having no idea he was dealing in drugs. Ashcroft was jailed in April 2002 for four and a half years after pleading guilty to being concerned in the supply of drugs and possessing a gun. The judge heard how Ashcroft used the family home where Gerrard had stayed as a safe house to store 5,000 Ecstasy tablets with a street value of up to £50,000. Lauren's mum, Jeanette, said, 'When Lauren began seeing Steven, she didn't even tell us at first. We couldn't believe it when Steven Gerrard walked down the path. But when he came in, he was a really down-to-earth fella, no airs or graces. Steven and her dad, Peter, got on really well. He was comfortable. Steven was always the perfect gentleman. Before they went on dates, he would ask permission from Lauren's dad. Of course, we were worried a bit, because it was Lauren's first serious boyfriend. But he phoned to tell me that he thought a lot about her.'

However, after three months the romance fizzled out as a result of Gerrard's trips away with his club and England. Even so, Gerrard, ever the gentleman, still kept in touch with Lauren and her family. But the continued friendship made Bromley go mad. The young thug was convinced the star was trying to steal his girlfriend, although Lauren told him he was just visiting her dad. After the first threats, Gerrard became worried about his safety and Lauren's. He gave a statement to the police about the car attack and asked them to protect Lauren, as he feared both of their lives could be in danger. In response, the police sent regular car patrols to Lauren's house and gave the family an emergency-hotline number to call in the event of an attack.

The intimidation escalated when Bromley spotted Gerrard driving in his car in Liverpool. Drawing up alongside him, he challenged Gerrard to fight him on the spot and threatened him with violence. But the footballer refused to stop and, after a high-speed car chase, gave him the slip.

Gerrard's troubles with Bromley became common knowledge

in Liverpool's underworld. The rumours went into overdrive when Bromley became embroiled in a gangland war unrelated to his vendetta with Gerrard, and two attempts were made on his life, both totally unconnected to the footballer. In April 2002, he was shot in the face by two men with sawn-off shotguns. Bodybuilder Bromley was peppered with gunshots, and pellets were embedded in his mouth and tongue. Fearing for his life, he discharged himself from hospital a day later. Just weeks later, he was attacked from behind in a Liverpool bar, where he was left for dead after suffering multiple injuries, including a broken jaw and nose. Close to death, he was eventually found and rushed to hospital, where he recovered in intensive care. Bromley, then 19, was sent to a young offenders institute in May 2002, after he admitted supplying heroin and crack cocaine as part of his general underworld dealings.

After seeing Lauren, I knocked on the door of Bromley's family home in the Tuebrook area of Liverpool to get his side of the story. But he was in jail on unrelated drugs convictions. However, his mother decided to speak on his behalf, to confirm some of the details. To her, Bromley was still her son and was being victimised for the sins of his father. With great difficulty, she tried to show him in the best possible light.

But the facts spoke for themselves. The Bromley family were well known to the police. His father, feared gangster George Bromley Senior, was executed in a gangland hit at the home of former armed robber and contract killer Charlie Seiga in 1997. Police accused one of Britain's top assassins of helping to do the job: All charges against Seiga in connection with this were dropped.

Following proudly in his father's footsteps, Bromley Junior became one of the youngest criminals in Britain to have assets seized by the courts when a Liverpool judge placed a confiscation order on the tearaway, forcing him to hand over £3,950. It is believed by underworld sources that he is in danger today. 'Someone has had two pops at him, so he will have to be careful,' one said. 'He fell for Lauren hook, line and sinker, and they were very close, but it was a stormy relationship because of his lifestyle. He had the money, the cars and a growing reputation as a hard-man, but he upset the big underworld names in Liverpool and he's now a marked man.'

Now I had nearly enough to run the story. For extra info, I rang the security boss of the property company who managed Gerrard's flat. He told me that a new alarm system had been installed as a result of the threats and how the police had been around to check security and had made arrangements to watch the premises closely. I got back to my room at the Moat House Hotel, ordered some prawn sarnies on room service, put on the little kettle in my room and began to write the story on my laptop.

It splashed in the *Sunday Mirror* on 9 February 2003, under the front-page headline 'EXCLUSIVE: DEATH THREATS TO ENGLAND STAR: He was protected by armed police'.

There was a twist in the tale which we never published. Before Bromley went to jail, he was forced to back off from Gerrard – not as a result of police intervention, but due to a couple of fairy godfathers who came to Gerrard's rescue, without him knowing what was going on.

Liverpool Football Club has a vast global following – but one set of fans are particularly interesting. They have no name, but they do have a common bond: the underworld. Most of them are rich, successful gangsters originally from Liverpool who now live abroad. Some of them are on the run from serious violent crimes they've committed. Others are known or wanted international drug-traffickers. Some of them live abroad because of the business advantages, in drug-hubs such as Amsterdam, Spain and South Africa, where they make more money selling drugs than they can in the UK due to the reduced risk level. Or they run money-laundering or forgery rackets. Some of the set live abroad because they have bought legitimate foreign businesses. Others simply travel the world, moving from one luxury hotel to another, playing golf and enjoying the fruits of their dishonesty.

But wherever they are, whatever they are doing, they will drop everything when Liverpool are playing in Europe. For Champions League games, they fly into whichever city the game is at, book into the best hotels and go to the match. Thousands of pounds are lavished on banquet meals, champagne on tap and prostitutes.

A former member of a Liverpool pop band who has followed Liverpool all over Europe since he was a child recalled how he met the shadowy group at a foreign hotel. He said, 'I was with a well-known ticket tout who took me into the hotel bar where they were staying. He turned around and said to me, "Everyone in this bar is a drug-dealer. Every single one is a grafter." They were Scousers living abroad who'd flown in from all over the world. Tickets were being bought at £500 a throw. There was a lot of snorting, brasses, all that carry on.'

One subset of the group includes men originally from the same area as Steven Gerrard. The Huyton squadron consists of infamous, long-standing and fantastically wealthy mass cannabis smugglers who mainly live in Amsterdam.

An international sports journalist who covers many of Liverpool's European games for British and foreign national papers has got to know the narco jet-set fans from staying at the same hotels. He said, 'They are an extraordinary group who float around the world but only come together for Liverpool games. Before a game, they don't communicate with each other to make arrangements. Phone calls are kept to a minimum, for obvious reasons. They just pick the best hotel wherever the game is and get in there. It's almost like a sixth sense that they know where the others will be. The hotels are even better than where the players are. It's all about £5,000-a-night suites and £2,000-a-go Chinese meals. In a hotel in Germany, I had a bottle of Cristal champagne given to me to drink by myself. Their wealth is obscene. Everything is one-upmanship, from clothes to cars to houses. When I told one that his Rolex was good, he took it off and said that I could have it and that he had another exactly like it back home, that he'd bought two that were robbed for next to nothing. I refused.

'Another man said that he'd just flown in from a safari in South Africa. He told me that, as he was checking into his jungle hotel, Patrick Swayze was in front of him and his wife in the queue. When he got to the reception, he asked which room Swayze was staying in and said that he wanted one the same or better. It was grands and grands a night, but he wouldn't be outdone by a Hollywood star.

'Loads of them live in Amsterdam. There's a part of it like a little Huyton because there's so many lads who live there.'

Members of the Huyton contingent came to Gerrard's rescue, completely without his say-so, or even his knowledge, during his dispute with Bromley. When they heard of Gerrard's trouble, they put a contract worth £30,000 on Bromley's head. The contract was taken up by two brothers from north Liverpool. They captured Bromley in a bar, tortured him and shot him at close range with a shotgun. The incident was referred to in the *Sunday Mirror* article, but no link was made between the shooting and Gerrard.

Two years later, in November 2005, I revealed in the *Sunday Mirror* how Gerrard could rest freely for the next ten years after Bromley was jailed again for an unconnected offence. Following in his father's footsteps, Bromley was jailed for torturing a drug-dealer with an iron.

GERRARD TERROR GANGSTER CAGED
Evil crook's mob tortured victims . . . with an IRON

A GANGLAND torturer who terrorised England star Steven Gerrard for four years has been jailed.

Evil George Bromley Junior made death threats against the Liverpool captain, his girlfriend and his family during a campaign of hate.

Bromley's gang is notorious in the underworld for following through on their threats – often by burning their victims with a red-hot iron.

After Bromley chased the 25-year-old midfielder through the streets of Liverpool in his car, police were drafted in to protect the soccer star.

But Gerrard, who earns £60,000 a week, breathed a sigh of

relief last week after Bromley – the son of a murdered gang boss – was jailed for ten years for leading a heroin ring.

Two of his enforcers were also convicted of torturing a drugs courier with an iron. They got the idea from Bromley's father, who 'ironed' the groins of drug-dealers who refused to pay him protection money. George Bromley Senior was later assassinated in a revenge hit.

An underworld source told the *Sunday Mirror*, 'Bromley has been on Gerrard's case for almost as long as he's been a big name at Liverpool.

'It was not a case of if but when something dangerous happened to Gerrard. Bromley is a psycho.'

Wayne Rooney carrying his shoes and clobber, just as he did on a fateful night out on Liverpool's Aigburth Road. (© *Liverpool Echo*)

Peter McIntosh, the football agent who first signed up
Wayne Rooney, and sports executive John Hyland.
(© Northpics)

Kenny Dalglish organised a meeting over the rights to control
Wayne Rooney's financial affairs at which Adams, the leader
of north London's notorious A-Team, was present.
(© *Liverpool Echo*)

Wayne Rooney's agent Paul Stretford, with brown envelope and bag. Neither of them contain bungs. However, the former vacuum-cleaner salesman was accused of trying to buy off the men who discovered the boy wonder with a £250,000 bag of readies. (© Northpics)

Businessman John Hyland arriving at court to launch a £10-million lawsuit against Rooney's under-fire agent Paul Stretford. (© Northpics)

Steven Gerrard: never say die. The Liverpool and England hero has weathered threats from gangsters for five years using the same indomitable spirit that makes him one of the few players who can turn lost games around as if by a miracle. (© Northpics)

Rio Ferdinand is shown the red card for behaving badly. His name was dragged through the courts because of associating unwittingly with a kidnapping gangster called Reds and a rapist dubbed The Predator.
(© Northpics)

Gangsta-chic. Michael Owen adopts the 'going to court' look – complete with posse – favoured by some of the villains he used to know. (© Northpics)

Switched-on Robbie Fowler has amassed a whopping fortune from his property-business empire, enabling him to shop at Cricket, the most famous WAGS clothing shop on the planet. (© Northpics)

'Who put this thing together? Wardy, that's who. Who do I trust? Wardy, that's who.' Mark Ward re-enacting his favourite scene from *Scarface*, with moody looks and double-breasted suit. (© *Liverpool Echo*)

The former Liverpool footballer Stephen Cole came to a gruesome and tragic end after he became a security boss when his footballing career was finished. (© Northpics)

5

Steven Gerrard: Moving to Chelsea . . . Can Damage Your Health

Troubled Stevie Gerrard suffered a second round of death threats from a totally different set of gangsters when he tried to move to Chelsea in 2004.

Just as the Bromley saga was subsiding and Gerrard was able to sleep tight in his bed again, the underworld began to cast a dark shadow over his life once more.

One furious gangster boasted that he would shoot Gerrard's foot off if he took the poisoned chalice of Abramovich's £30-million fee and £120,000-a-week pay packet.

Others warned that they would attack Gerrard's family – including his long-term partner Alex Curran, the mother of their newly born baby.

This time, the gangsters' motive wasn't money or love or blackmail – it was a sense of betrayal. Fanatical elements in the underworld felt that Gerrard was turning his back on the club he loved – for thirty pieces of silver, not thirty million quid. What's more, he was seen as trading with the enemy. Casting off a sacred privilege in favour of Chelsea's super-rich flash-Harry owner Roman Abramovich was seen as a biblical betrayal. Words like Judas and Barabbas began to appear on Internet message boards.

FOOTBALL AND GANGSTERS

It's easy to understand why Liverpool fans were so destructively protective of their team captain. Gerrard was a home-grown product of the Liverpool Youth Academy. His passion was the driving force behind Anfield's rebirth, from the wilderness years back into the big-time, which began around 2000. When he is at the top of his game, Liverpool more than usually win. He is considered by many to be the complete midfield player, one of the few players in the world who has the mettle to drag a team back from defeat against horrific odds, as he did in the Champions League final in 2005 and the FA Cup final in 2006. The former YTS trainee Gerrard made his Reds debut in November 1998 as a second-half substitute against Blackburn. His full debut came in the UEFA Cup against Celta Vigo. From the off, his outstanding performance belied his tender years.

Gerrard lived the dream of the born-and-bred Scouser playing for his club. Never afraid to go in for a tackle, he made rapid progress. His on-the-pitch vision left opponents stunned, and Gerrard scored spectacular goals. His strike against Manchester United during the 2000–01 Treble season was voted the club's best-ever Premiership goal. His mantlepiece soon began to fill up, as he collected winners' medals in the Worthington Cup (twice), FA Cup and UEFA Cup, and the PFA Young Player of the Year award in 2001. Anfield legend Kevin Keegan handed Gerrard his England debut, and the midfielder scored his first goal for his country in Munich with a magnificent strike from 25 yards in the legendary 5–1 win over Germany in September 2001.

But from then on, life began to get complicated. Success and growing up had its downsides. Gerrard was unable to break free of his working-class upbringing. And equally, some of the rougher elements were not going to allow him to. He was still a bit of a scally at heart – he could fight – and he didn't realise that continuing to live as he had always done amongst a few baddies was going to lead to trouble. He soon had that first brush with the underworld in the form of George Bromley Junior.

In the Premiership, Liverpool's resurgence began to falter as Gerard Houllier's sheen began to wear off. More significantly, Russian billionaire oligarch Roman Abramovich had turned the League table on its head. His £250-million injection into Chelsea meant that Liverpool might never attain the success they were striving for. Abramovich's arrival effectively turned the Premiership into a big-club apartheid, with Chelsea, Man United and Arsenal playing against themselves and the rest of the League condemned to a tournament between must-try-harder second-raters. And Stevie G would have known it. As a desperate-for-success, ambitious, world-class player, it seemed he wasn't going to settle for less, Scouse heritage or no Scouse heritage.

In 2004, Gerrard returned from the European Championship as an England hero alongside Wayne Rooney. He had tasted pan-global adulation for the first time, and pundits noted it might be hard for him to let it ebb away, playing for what some commentators were now describing as a journeyman team, in what they were predicting was rapidly becoming a backwater club, saddled with what appeared to be a weary management. The writing was on the wall. The talk-radio phone-ins were awash with the bitter tears of bewildered Liverpool fans. Gerrard wasn't going to hang around until the wheels came off.

Chelsea had approached Gerrard before the Euro 2004 tournament. It's easy to imagine that such a deal would have occupied much of his thoughts during the Championship. It is said he sent a text message to new Chelsea manager José Mourinho within hours of the fateful penalty-shoot-out defeat, saying how much he was looking forward to moving to Stamford Bridge. Gerrard had seemingly become disillusioned with Liverpool. The club had not increased the terms of the four-year contract their star player had signed the previous November. Gerrard, it was said, secretly believed that they didn't want him anyway. Once he was back in the UK, negotiations with Chelsea got under way. Abramovich offered a £30-million transfer fee and to double his £60,000-a-week wages. Gerrard agreed.

In his youth, Gerrard would have seen a legendary strip of graffiti written on a tiled wall outside Lime Street train station. The spray-canned words read 'Ordinary to Chelsea'. It was a cryptic boast by some of Liverpool's Urchin gang about the elite coolness of travelling to Stamford Bridge on an InterCity train – an ordinary rattler – as opposed to a football special, dressed in their finest exotic sportswear, so avoiding the police monitoring which would have prevented them engaging Chelsea fans in violent acts of football hooliganism. Ironically, Steven Gerrard was about to find out how the lads who wrote this graffiti in the late '70s and early '80s felt about his plans, whether he was moving to Chelsea by ordinary, special or Roman Abramovich's private 747.

Immediately, there was a mass outcry from the fans. How could the player who tried to persuade Michael Owen to rebuke Real Madrid and stay at Anfield now follow in his footsteps? An underworld source said, 'There is a gangster in Cantril Farm who threatened to shoot him in the foot if he goes to Chelsea. A meeting was called in a pub. There were several well-known fellas, including some senior doormen. Someone who was close to Gerrard was told to come down, and these fellers put him under manners. "Tell Steven that if he goes to Chelsea, we will fucking batter him." Then one of them said he will make sure he never fucking plays again. That he will cap him [shoot him]. This man said he would put one in his foot. There was no laughing. He was serious.

'What you have got to understand is that this is not just about mad fans. It's more complicated. There are several things going on. Of course, all of these lads have followed Liverpool since they were this high and they don't want to lose one of their own to the likes of Abramovich. They don't like him, because their attitude is money can't buy you the history of something like Liverpool Football Club. You can't buy love – that kind of thing. These lads want success from their club.

'But there are other things as well. These fellas do it because they can. They like the fact that they have an input into these big decisions. They can only do it because they are the main lads where Stevie grew up and they think they can control him to some degree by threatening him or his family. Everyone in the city is talking about who said what to who. Certain fellas are being treated as heroes, because everyone is saying things like, "He's the man who stopped Gerrard going to Chelsea," as though he's done the city a favour or something.

'The next thing is that there is a lot of money riding on this. A lot of people make a living off the club, directly and indirectly. Think about it: there's touts; there's security; the businesses around the ground; all the firms which sell things to the club; the nightclubs where the players go and bring in the people; there's the players' wages themselves supporting a lot of behaviour; people doing things for them, you know what I mean; there's people who make dough out of selling them houses; they lend people money to start businesses; they invest in local things. The bottom line is that the club has been there for a hundred fucking years, and a lot of people's livings are riding on it. So they are not going to let some fucking Russian tycoon who's already Brewstered come in and queer the pitch. If that means having a word with a player, then so be it.'

Days after the record-breaking transfer was announced, everything mysteriously changed. Gerrard told a press conference that he had decided to remain at Liverpool. But he was clearly rattled, some observers noted. On camera, he looked shell-shocked, and his answers were monosyllabic rather than over the moon. The performance didn't look like a celebration, more like resignation to the facts of life in modern football. Gerrard said, 'I have gone with my heart and decided to stay. I love this club and the supporters, and that's what it boils down to.'

What had happened in between to change Gerrard's mind? Insiders claim that a visit from his father, Paul, to his son's home in Liverpool turned the midfielder's world upside down. Paul Gerrard had previously been behind his son's move to Stamford Bridge. The initial threats from non-underworld fanatical supporters had been dismissed as hollow. But at that fateful meeting, Paul had a stark message for his son: you can't go to Chelsea. Paul told his son that, despite the gold and glory, he had to consider the people he would be leaving behind. If he left Liverpool, life for the Gerrard family would become intolerable.

In the face of such pressure, the man renowned for never pulling out of a tackle buckled. The Chelsea deal was derailed. For the sake of his family, Gerrard would stay. A more sinister force had made it so.

FOOTBALL AND GANGSTERS

Despite his decision to stay at the club, the threats continued. Like blackmailers who get paid off, the gangsters continued to harass Gerrard, encouraged that they had forced a result. But it was no secret that Chelsea were still interested, and Gerrard still had his eye on the ball. To keep the pressure up, the underworld now turned on his partner and baby daughter. Worried Gerrard began to fear for their safety. He told Alex that she had to 'watch her back at all times' when she ventured out alone. The gangsters believed that she was the easiest way of getting to him.

The first threats were circulated among a small band of fanatics around March 2005, but word soon reached Gerrard's and Alex's families. Her concerned mother, Kim, said that it was a terrifying time for her daughter.

Clearly worried that talking about the threats would make the situation worse, she added, 'I don't want to say anything about that, but certainly Alex doesn't want or deserve this kind of thing.'

The £3-million mansion they shared in Crosby, north Liverpool, began to resemble a fortress, with 10-ft-high iron gates and state-of-the-art security cameras. Gerrard enlisted the services of four heavies to protect them when they were there.

A pal said, 'Steven's really worried at the moment. You can't just forget it when people say they'll do you and your family harm if you leave Liverpool. He's had a run-in with these sort before and he knows they mean business.'

Some of the new threats came from wannabe gangsters out to impress old enemy George Bromley Junior, who was now out of prison.

A source said, 'Word's gone out that Gerrard's not to leave Anfield in any circumstances. A small group has made it their mission to make sure he stays, and they'll do whatever. It's not Georgie Bromley's doing but people who know him and want respect.'

Bromley's manor is one of the most dangerous ganglands in Britain. A pal of Gerrard's said, 'Steve knows what these people are like, and that's why he's so worried. His world would fall apart if anything ever happened to those he loves.'

Gerrard thought about hiring ex-special forces bodyguards for Alex but instead made sure that the car he bought her – a £55,000 BMW 645 convertible – was toughened with reinforced steel. As a further security measure, he asked Alex to stay away from Liverpool city centre and go out in Manchester instead, where she would be less recognised.

Worried or not, the ever-professional Gerrard got on with the job and took Liverpool and England to greater heights. England qualified for the World Cup. Two months after the death threats, in May 2005, he captained Liverpool to their fifth European Cup, against AC Milan in Istanbul. The game was an unbelievable roller-coaster of football drama – settled after extra time with sudden-death pens. But it was Gerrard's unrelenting, steely spirit, coupled with his talent and controlled aggression, that won the game. What he had, you couldn't bottle. It wasn't long before Abramovich came sniffing round again.

Extremists vowed to 'do anything' to keep Gerrard at Liverpool. Messages left on an Internet forum used by the notorious Urchins firm made it clear to Gerrard that if he left, he would *never* be allowed to return to his native city. Some even asked teammate Jamie Carragher to 't**t him'. One read: 'He will have to move out of the city and disappear for good. No more old mates, no more school mates, no more family visits and nights out in town.' Of course, Carragher did not follow the advice.

Another read: 'He's a slimy f*****g weasel mercenary t**t.'

One underworld figure said feelings were running so high that some were prepared to 'take action', adding, 'The thought of him quitting to go to Chelsea was a red rag. Let's just say anything might have been done to keep him at the club.'

6

Rio Ferdinand: Rude Boys

England stars Rio Ferdinand and Michael Duberry had their reputations dragged through the courts because of their brief run-in with a heroin dealer and a serial rapist dubbed The Predator.

The story is a modern cautionary tale to all young footballers of how gangsters can subtly penetrate a player's inner circle – then get him into trouble just by being there.

Gangsters and footballers often flirt with each other socially, mainly because their lives overlap in places like nightclubs, and often because they have the same interests: namely, women, money, status and good times.

Young footballers often enjoy the adulation from these mysterious, powerful men, who are as much celebrities in their own communities as they are. And gangsters love to hang around footy stars in case some of the glitz rubs off on them. They love to be in the company of successful people, because it often reaffirms their insecure view of their own achievements. And because there might be money to be made.

Either way, members of the underworld find it easy to hang around the edges of players' entourages, and often the players aren't aware of the risks involved. The relationship can become twisted. Some criminals become obsessed with trying to impress or please their new associates

– often with warped consequences. Ferdinand's case is a classic example of how some footballers' brush with the dark side can end in tears and tragedy.

As always, there are two sides to the story. When this tale first came to light, in a criminal trial, the court was told how Ferdinand struck up a relationship with a 37-year-old gangster called Michael Archibald, a gun-toting drug-dealer known on the street as Reds because of the colour of his flashy BMW. He later became Ferdinand's minder and nightclub chaperone, the footballer not knowing about his criminal links. On one particular night out, a girl was sexually assaulted. The attacker was a friend of Archibald's, an underworld hanger-on, who had been motivated to do the attack after she turned down the sexual advances of Rio Ferdinand, or so the prosecution claimed.

The other side of the story, as told by Ferdinand and Duberry, was that the case was nothing to do with them and that their links to gangsters had been fabricated and their behaviour exaggerated in a bid to help supply the defendant with a preposterous defence.

At the time, Ferdinand, then 24, and Duberry, then 26, were the golden boys at Leeds, when the club was still a world-renowned Premiership team awash with cash and top-rate players, before its demise into financial oblivion under the weight of the sky-high wage bill and the chairmanship of spend-king Peter Ridsdale. The players should have been keeping a low profile. Only a few months before, teammates Lee Bowyer and Jonathan Woodgate had dragged the whiter-than-white Leeds shirt through the mud after being accused of beating up an Asian student in a seedy, booze-fuelled brawl. Though the pair were eventually acquitted of committing grievous bodily harm against Sarfraz Najeib, Woodgate was found guilty of affray. The fallout from the ten-week, multimillion-pound trial left a bitter aftertaste in the mouths of many fans, and questions were being asked about the falling standards of behaviour among many of the game's best-known players.

But despite the controversy, nothing was going to stop Ferdinand and Duberry having a good time. They regularly shared a party-filled boys' night out, often hitting the bars once or twice a week if there wasn't a midweek game. On the night in question, Ferdinand and Duberry went into town at about 8.00. After sharing a bottle of wine, the stars ended up in the Hi-Fi nightclub, where they began knocking back drinks with convicted kidnapper Archibald. Duberry had known Reds for about two years, but later claimed that he didn't know of his underworld reputation. Ferdinand had also known Reds for a while, after meeting him in a back-street Caribbean restaurant in the Chapeltown area of the city.

Fuelled by several glasses of vodka and Red Bull, Ferdinand and Duberry started doing what cocky young footy players like to do best – chatting up women. There were plenty of opportunities – they were standing in a narrow corridor near the ladies' toilets and girls were forced to run the gauntlet through the star-studded entourage if they wanted to use the loo. But, in true ghetto-ladulous footballer style, their chat-up technique left a lot to be desired – and a number of girls angry and distressed, or so they claimed later. Several women complained to nightclub staff that they'd been pestered by the two footballers. By this time, Ferdinand was on the Baileys and ice. One girl claimed that defender Duberry put his hand up her skirt, forcing her to fight him off by slapping him – an allegation which he strenuously denied. But she eventually calmed down, she said, and stayed with the group. Ominously, she was the girl who was later sexually assaulted by another member of the group. At about midnight – four hours after the players had started drinking – Duberry and the future £30-million Manchester United defender Ferdinand allegedly took a woman clubber into the gents' loos, an incident which the footballers did not recall. Whatever the truth, an independent witness in the form of a bouncer said he caught the trio just as they were about to lock the door on the cubicle. Doorman David Whittaker said he burst into the toilet and found all three inside the cubicle. He told Leeds Crown Court: 'They were about to close the door. I managed to stop them and told them and the girl to go.

'The girl said something like, "They tried to take me in." I cannot

107

remember her being distressed. I spoke to Ferdinand and Duberry and told them they should know better.'

The duo eventually left the club with the villain Reds and two women, one of whom would later be assaulted. Outside, Ferdinand, who was 24 at the time, jumped on the roof of a stranger's Land Rover Discovery. Prosecutor Richard Newbury said he had to be dragged off by another footballer: Bradford City striker Isaiah Rankin. The two then started scuffling. Duberry and Ferdinand finally piled into Reds's Range Rover and went to the plush four-star Oulton Hall Hotel on the outskirts of the city . . . along with the two women they'd met in the club.

At about 2.30 a.m., Ferdinand and Duberry, the two women and Reds piled into a room and shared two bottles of champagne. Despite being with the nightclub ladies, Ferdinand phoned his girlfriend. Afterwards, one of the women later claimed that she had rejected his advances and that angry Ferdinand had threatened to get someone to slap her, which Ferdinand denied. The court heard how the exchange was overheard by Reds, who acted unilaterally to avenge the snub. Prosecutors claimed that he ordered underling Martin Luther King, a cinema worker who was on bail accused of raping a prostitute in London, to follow the girl home and beat her up. King was later found guilty of dragging her into a car, after posing as a taxi driver, and attempting to rape her at gunpoint at a secluded spot whilst implying that the attack was retaliation for snubbing Ferdinand and upsetting Duberry. The woman, who cannot be named for legal reasons, claimed King told her, 'It's not me doing this – it's Michael and Rio.'

Miraculously, the woman managed to escape into a nearby wood, and after King had driven off she flagged down a car and went to the police. She remembered King's registration plate, and the following day he was arrested by armed police at his house. Ferdinand and Duberry were questioned by the police after the incident, but no charges were brought against either of them.

The use of the car, the gun and the deception made it similar to the rape King had carried out only a few months earlier and for which he was on bail. King had attacked a teenager in London after she'd agreed to take a ride with him. He raped the 17 year old after driving her to his home on the pretext of an interview to work in an escort agency he had set up. The teenager later told police that King threatened her at gunpoint with the words: 'If you want to be scared, I will scare you.' Luckily, the girl remembered the registration number of King's car. This number was later to match that of the car King was driving on the night of his assault in Leeds.

When the case got to court, Duberry played down his alleged hell-raising – and his relationship with Reds. He said he'd known Reds for two years, but only by his nickname. The former England Under-21 international said he didn't know he had a bad reputation. Prosecutor Richard Newbury said Reds was a 'serious criminal' and a 'violent man', who was a drug-dealer and kidnapper. He asked Duberry, 'Did he give you any hint he was part of the criminal underworld?'

The football star replied, 'The conversations we had never went deeper than football, music and clubs.'

Duberry admitted that he and Ferdinand had been 'boisterous' in the club and had been warned by a bouncer to 'calm down'. But he denied going into the gents' loos with his pal and a woman, or that he and Ferdinand had been ticked off by doormen on several occasions after different women complained about them. He told the court that, at the Hi-Fi club in Leeds, he and Ferdinand started drinking Baileys, plus vodka and Red Bulls. Duberry admitted, 'Everyone always had a drink in their hands.'

Mr Newbury claimed the players and their pals had deliberately stood in a corridor leading to the ladies' loos so that women would have to weave between them. Duberry said, 'We did stand there, but we were in other parts of the club, too.'

The prosecutor alleged that Duberry and Ferdinand got their first warning from a doorman just before midnight, after a woman complained about them. Duberry said, 'I don't recall that. I remember a bouncer coming over to me and Rio and saying, "Just calm down a bit."'

He went on to say that he couldn't remember his pal Ferdinand getting involved in any further trouble.

During the trial, Ferdinand was banned from driving for six months, fined £2,500 and ordered to pay costs of £3,000 for speeding arising from an earlier and unrelated offence. He had been caught doing 92 mph on the M1 in his Cadillac Escalade the previous year.

Ferdinand had left his England colleagues training for a vital Euro 2004 qualifier against Turkey on the day he took the witness stand. Before he gave evidence, Ferdinand was told by Judge Scott Wolstenholme, 'You are not obliged to answer a question if your answering will incriminate you of a criminal offence.' Prosecutor Richard Newbury said there was no suggestion that he had ordered the abduction, but his 'minder', Reds, may have overheard his clash with the girl and acted on it.

'I'm not suggesting necessarily you instructed anyone to go and smack this girl up,' he said. 'It would have been sufficient that Reds or his friend in the car had seen this incident.'

Ferdinand said, 'No.'

Mr Newbury went on: 'He was there to sort things out for you, wasn't he?'

'No.'

But Ferdinand did admit he knew Reds and had met him in bars, at matches and in a back-street West Indian food kitchen in Chapeltown, Leeds, where he went for meals. But Mr Newbury accused the footballer of playing down his relationship with Reds – who was really his minder and had supplied a girl for him. Ferdinand denied it and insisted the girls had simply been in Reds's car when he climbed in.

The prosecutor asked, 'Did you know Reds has a history of serious criminal convictions?'

Ferdinand was emphatic. 'No,' he said. Furthermore, Ferdinand denied that he knew of Reds's connection to drug-dealing, violence and kidnapping or that he'd ever met Reds's unsavoury associate King.

Ferdinand's and Duberry's claims did not impress the prosecutor. He accused the stars of lying in court to save their careers. In their defence, however, the judge found no impropriety, nor did he comment on the value of their evidence. In his final speech to the jury, Richard Newbury told them the footballers were a 'side issue' which King had decided to play. 'They are not on trial, and this case is not about them,' he said. 'The centre of this case is what happened between the 21-year-old woman and Martin Luther King, and the involvement of the footballers is peripheral to the case.'

Mr Newbury told the jury, 'They [Ferdinand and Duberry] have come to court and given their evidence and what value it is is a matter for you. You have to decide the usefulness of their evidence in deciding this case.' But he warned the jury, 'When you decide the value of it, keep your feet on the ground.'

The jury did, and King was convicted of attempted rape and indecent assault. King was described as an aggressive and domineering predator and given two life sentences. King had come to the UK in 1999. At his first trial in London, King was convicted of rape. The case could not be reported until after the Leeds hearing. Balbir Singh, in mitigation, said there was no evidence King would remain a danger.

Judge Scott Wolstenholme told King his victims were in fear of their lives. The Leeds woman, he said, had shown great courage in trying to escape from his car during a terror journey in which he became violent before sexually assaulting her.

'A doctor found 23 separate sites of injury on her body but those were minor compared to the emotional distress you inflicted on her. She was badly traumatised by her ordeal,' said the judge.

He said a report revealed King was a predatory rapist and a high risk to women. 'You are intelligent but also aggressive, domineering and manipulative,' the judge said.

He said King would not qualify for parole until he had been in prison for six and a half years, but added, 'You will not be released until the parole board is satisfied you are no longer a risk.' He recommended that King then be deported.

Detective Superintendent Howard Crowther, of West Yorkshire

FOOTBALL AND GANGSTERS

Police, praised the Leeds victim, who had to give evidence twice after King's first trial was aborted. 'She is satisfied justice has now been seen to be done,' he said.

A few months later, Reds was jailed for 11 years in connection with a separate case for cocaine-dealing and firearms offences. The court heard how Archibald had gained his nickname because he drove a red BMW car with the personalised plate RED 9. He traded in cocaine and heroin and could supply 'metal' – slang for firearms – and ammunition. Archibald's criminal activities were halted after undercover cops infiltrated his illegal activities and gained his trust. Gang members Mark Tolson and Jonathan Crumbie were also snared in the operation.

Archibald pleaded guilty to the supply and conspiracy to supply hard drugs, possession of a revolver and a Derringer pistol and ammunition.

Jailing them, Judge Peter Charlesworth said the evidence revealed Archibald was heavily involved in crime in Leeds. The judge commended the officers involved in the investigation, code-named Operation Primary, saying they worked in 'dangerous and difficult' circumstances.

Prosecutor Sean Morris said of Reds, 'He said Leeds was his town and he would let them know people worth knowing.'

The court cases had given the public a glimpse into the no-holds-barred, anything-goes social no-man's-land where soccer players and gangsters often meet – a place where all bets are off as regards standards of decent behaviour and a place where footballers can quickly get out of order if left unchecked. The case proved that football and gangsters are a dangerous mixture. Footballers seem to have an insatiable appetite for hedonism. Gangsters seem to be proud of their ability to supply their fantasies, even if they have reached their positions through violence and intimidation.

7

Leeds United: Cutting Costs by Drugging Players?

In the winter of 2005, I broke a big story about a bizarre plot to spike a soccer star's food and drink. Leeds United's £5-million defender Michael Duberry was apparently the intended victim in an alleged doping scam designed to deliberately wreck his career. A former Leeds executive, who claims he was in on the act, blew the whistle, claiming that the plan involved surreptitiously getting cocaine, Ecstasy or banned steroids into Duberry's system so he would fail a drugs test. The aim was to engineer the one-time England international's sacking, because the crisis-hit Championship club could no longer afford to pay his £24,000-a-week salary. Another plan, it was claimed, was to end the career of his fellow top-wage earner Gary Kelly, then 30, by hiring hit men to break his legs. Finally, another stranger-than-fiction plot was hatched to drug opponents Coventry City and their high-profile manager, former Leeds boss Peter Reid, by lacing a pre-match banquet with Ecstasy. The plots and schemes followed the £22-million takeover of Leeds by a Yorkshire-based consortium in March 2004 after the financial problems which Leeds has suffered since the departure of former spendaholic chairman Peter Ridsdale. To refinance the debt-ridden club, the new owners wanted to sell the ground and slash the £15-million wage bill.

The Leeds affair was one of the weirdest stories I have ever worked on. I was supposed to be probing some of the senior bosses at one of Britain's biggest and most well-respected clubs. Leeds may have dropped out of the Premiership due to the financial earthquake that hit Elland Road, but its worldwide fan base is mind-bogglingly large, loyal and potentially lucrative. Chairman Peter Ridsdale had controversially resigned two years earlier in 2003, leaving the club a whopping £103 million in debt. However, during the investigation involving the new regime, what I found was more like a Shakespeare play than a normal business, full of clever, manipulative characters who seemed to revel in stabbing each other in the back whilst engaged in fantastic, hare-brained get-rich-quick schemes. I'd been around the block several times as a Fleet Street reporter, but I never expected to find what I unearthed in this boardroom.

If some of the sources were to be believed, then several gangsters were involved in the plans. For instance, gangsters had allegedly been drafted in as heavies. And several former football hooligans turned underworld bosses were involved in negotiations to take over the club or lend their support to favourable bidders. But the real point of the story wasn't that businessmen had hired underworld figures to do their dirty work, but that, if true, the businessmen *themselves* had adopted a criminal mindset to problem-solving and had adopted gangster tactics *themselves* to achieve their goals.

The whistle-blower was the former Leeds executive Chris Middleton, a security-company owner turned property developer who was parachuted into Elland Road to look after the interests of the senior director Simon Morris, who led the consortium that had taken over the ailing club. Middleton claimed that the various plots to nobble players were hatched between himself and the Aston Martin-driving Morris, though he now regretted being involved, claiming that he had acted under duress. According to Middleton, 'Simon was clever. He would never demand something; he would leave it to your judgement. But if it didn't happen, he would become agitated. He wanted me to drug him, do something. He left it to me.' Of course, the story soon degenerated into a tit-for-tat row between Middleton's camp and Morris's supporters, with claim and counter-claim and everybody blaming each other for wrongdoing and attempting to discredit the other side. Morris denied being involved in any plan to sabotage Duberry and Kelly and slagged off Middleton for being a 'rogue employee' who was sacked for gross misconduct. Certainly, Middleton may have been unhappy with Morris, because he felt he had been badly treated as an employee at Leeds, and his evidence must be viewed bearing this in mind. But while the war of words raged on, the sordid affair did have some wider benefit, in as much as it allowed the paying public a ringside seat to the behind-the-scenes goings-on at a modern football club, where cash is king in the boardroom and the underworld influence is never far away.

Three witnesses to the extraordinary plan gave me testimonies corroborating the events, though they cannot all be described as credible. And former Leeds operations manager Middleton, who was now ashamed of his part in the plot, admitted his role. Middleton claimed they planned to sprinkle powdered drugs disguised as Parmesan cheese on Duberry's pasta dish whilst he enjoyed a meal at one of Leeds's top restaurants. He says that he and Morris – then a 28-year-old property millionaire and life-long Leeds fan – also considered dissolving banned steroids in a sports protein drink aimed at the former Chelsea defender. Morris later rubbished the claims, saying, 'None of these things ever happened. I have no knowledge of the serious allegations.'

Whatever the truth, Middleton claimed the idea arose from a chat the men had about reducing the wage bill at the cash-strapped club in March 2004. He said they originally discussed trying to arrange for defender Kelly to fail an alcohol breath test. But then Middleton claims the conversation, held at Morris's property-business office in Leeds a few months later in the summer of 2004, turned to Duberry. Middleton said, 'I was there with another businessman, who would later form part of a consortium to buy the club. Morris and I planned to spike Duberry.

Morris made out there were four major liabilities on the players' wage bill: Eirik Bakke, Michael Duberry, Gary Kelly and Seth Johnson. He wanted to cut costs by getting these players off the wage bill. He made it clear that their wages were in excess of £10 million a year. Johnson and Bakke were untouchable because they were injured. The basis was Gary Kelly to start with. The boss [Morris] knew Kelly went to the Bingley Arms every night. He said, "Can we breath-test him?" Morris then moved on to Duberry. There was talk about drugging his meal at a restaurant in Leeds called Bibi's during a team meal, putting something in his drink, all sorts of stuff. Me and Morris planned to do it.'

Middleton was a streetwise 25 year old and he phoned his contacts in the underworld to find out which drugs stayed in the bloodstream long enough to fail a dope test. He claimed he played along with the plan to please Morris but had no intention of carrying it out. He said, 'Morris would get annoyed and ask what was happening. I was always making excuses. The plan changed to trying to lace sports drinks with steroids, because he came to the conclusion that it wasn't safe to do it at a restaurant. A call went in to the Leeds manager Kevin Blackwell suggesting they look at giving the players protein drinks to improve their conditioning.' Blackwell was not part of the plot, but his permission was needed to introduce the new drinks into the sports regime.

Middleton researched how to source 50-mg capsules of banned steroids to put in Duberry's and Kelly's protein drinks after training. He said, 'But then Blackwell opposed the idea of getting protein drinks and that, and it went out of the window.'

Morris confirmed there had been a plan to introduce protein drinks for the players. But he said it was to reduce the weight of unfit players and nothing to do with a drug sting. Feeling betrayed and disgusted, he added once again, 'I deny plotting the Gary Kelly allegations.' To back up his rebuttal, the entrepreneur did what he does best. He attempted to demolish the claims by using business logic. 'It doesn't make economic sense. If he's in hospital for four weeks, it's going to cost you a hundred grand. He's on twenty-four grand a week. It's nonsense.'

LEEDS UNITED: CUTTING COSTS BY DRUGGING PLAYERS?

A Leeds businessman did come forward to confirm that he had witnessed the first meeting between Morris and Middleton where the Duberry drug plot was hatched. The businessman was a former top boy in Leeds's notorious hooligan Service Crew. He was able to use his hooligan power base as a strong influence at Leeds and he was privy to much insider-dealing at the club. The Service Crew man said, 'They said, "We'll go somewhere in Leeds where we can get hold of the chef, put something in Michael Duberry's food and then hopefully we can get him off the payroll."'

Another witness was sports investment broker Paul Garland. He was being paid £2,000 a week to help refinance the club and was negotiating with an American sports investment firm called Nova to invest in Leeds. Garland's testimony must also be viewed carefully. He is a convicted fraudster and a former bankrupt, and the *Sunday Mirror* paid him for his story. Whatever the value of his statement, in it Garland claims that Morris revealed his plans to dope Duberry at a meeting in Garland's house on 18 September 2004. Garland said, 'I explained one of the concerns of the investors Nova was about some of the higher-paid players, including Michael Duberry, Gary Kelly, Seth Johnson and Eirik Bakke. Their wages were substantially greater than most of the Leeds players – they made up 45 per cent of the total Leeds United Football Club [LUFC] wage bill. Morris said that there were "ways of dealing with this". He said he had friends who "might tip the wink that he had taken something" and the club would get him tested the next day and terminate his contract. Morris said if that didn't work, "we will spike the drinks he has after training". I protested that this was disgraceful and that young players' careers ought not to be sabotaged in this way. Morris just laughed and said they were costing the club too much and "they are f***ing crap!"'

Another Leeds businessman – who was heading a different consortium to buy the club – also told of a plan to drug Duberry. The businessman said, 'I told Morris, "My consortium has £25 million, and the only way forward is to get back in the Premiership, but we haven't enough money.

You need a minimum of £45 million – and the big problem is obviously the wage bill you've inherited."

'We went on to talk about the wage contract and conditions. I said, "Who's going to take Gary Kelly on a transfer?"

'Morris said, "We'll probably just get his legs broke and then get the insurance money."

'Then Duberry was mentioned. I said, "What are you going to do with Duberry?"

'He said, "Wolves have shown an interest in him."

'I said, "Wolves are not going to take Duberry. They must know how bad he is."

'He then said, "Well, we could get him drugged."

'I'd heard this before, because a businessman pal had said they were going to get Duberry drugged and cancel his contract.'

Middleton also told of a plan to get Kelly off the payroll by breaking his legs and cashing in his lucrative insurance policy. Middleton said, 'Then Morris said, "What if we get him beaten up? I mean seriously beaten up." I had no answer. I conveniently forgot about it. I wanted no part in it. The boss was desperate. No one wanted to buy the club's main assets.'

In a separate meeting, Paul Garland claimed that the Leeds boss revealed his plans to put a contract on Kelly. Garland said, 'He said, "He is the easiest of the lot – we'll just have him done over in the car park of the pub. It would be the easiest thing in the world for a couple of Man United fans to beat him up and smash his legs, so that he'd never play again."

'I thought it was despicable. He was clearly anticipating an arranged serious physical attack on Gary Kelly to inflict serious injuries sufficient to end his football career.'

But Morris was not shaken. He resolutely stuck to his story that the whole fantastic caboodle was a concoction, a complete fabrication made up by greedy and disgruntled business associates who had not got what they wanted out of Leeds or had fairly and squarely come off worse than him in the world of commerce. In addition, they were jealous of his precocious success. He blasted his adversaries, saying of Middleton and Garland, 'If you lay down with dogs, you get fleas. All these guys piss in the same pot and have the same goal of causing disruption to Leeds United.'

If there wasn't already enough talk of nobbling and spiking, there was more to come. And it was even more outlandish. Whistle-blower Middleton claimed that Morris instructed him to nobble visiting Coventry City manager Peter Reid and his team. Again, Morris denied any role in this scheme, but Middleton said, 'The Peter Reid and Coventry situation arose after it was arranged for Reid and his team to go to a restaurant called Bibi's that night. Simon then phoned me and said, "Get down there, get some Es and put them in the drinks, because we are playing tomorrow."

'I went down, but I didn't get the drugs. Simon wanted me to spike the drinks. He thought it would be highly amusing if they couldn't play the next day. As it was, Leeds stuffed Coventry 3–1. I was a hero. Simon winked at me and patted me on the back. He thought I had administered the drug.'

No other Leeds directors were implicated in any of the plots. Middleton said the club tried to sack him for gross misconduct but that he eventually resigned with a £27,000 pay-off and a reference. Simon Morris – who later sold his stake to current owner Ken Bates – continued to hit back at the allegations made by Chris Middleton and the three other businessmen, claiming that they fabricated the story for their own ends. Morris said, 'These are total lies, and you cannot believe a word of it. Paul Garland wanted to get back at me and the club because he wasn't happy that his deal to buy Leeds didn't go through. He's a fraud. When I met Middleton, he was sleeping on his mother's couch. He didn't have a pot to piss in. I brought him in and this is the thanks I got. But when he got the job, he wanted more, but in my opinion he didn't do it right and he made mistakes. The bottom line is I wasn't interested in the betrayals and the infighting whilst I was at the club. I dedicated my life to saving the club when the pressure was on, when nobody else was prepared to take the risk, and worked every hour to help build it back up. I never took a penny out of that club. We had the backing of the fans, and we worked hard to repay them. But unfortunately some people just wanted to feather their own nest, take money out of the club and take advantage.'

However, the trouble for Morris kept coming despite his denials. He was accused of asking for bungs in excess of £1 million to smooth through any potential deals with investors – an accusation which Morris also denied.

The gangsters first started to circle when the club collapsed under Ridsdale – they could smell weakness; they could see an opportunity. Blackwell said of the darkest days, 'People think we were £80 million in debt. Well, the actual figure was £119 million, and an email came to my office telling me: "Some players might get paid; some might not." I tried to keep it from them for as long as possible, because it was embarrassing. I'd brought the players here and some had asked me beforehand if we were financially sound. I'd told them we were, but clearly I'd been misled.'

Many of their star players were sold off cheaply in a fire sale. Harry Kewell was valued at £7 million, but Leeds got only £2 million. England goalkeeper Paul Robinson went to Tottenham for a knock-down £1.5 million. Football financier Paul Garland was brought in by one of Morris's early business partners, Geoffrey Richmond, to help raise cash for the Yorkshire Consortium. When the club passed into Morris's hands, Garland was retained to help get the club back on its feet. But little did anyone know that Garland had just pulled off a huge fraud for which he was being investigated by police and would later be convicted. The Porsche-driving businessman was paid a consultancy fee of £2,000 a week by Leeds as the club battled to avoid financial oblivion in 2004. Even though the new bosses had successfully reduced the initial massive debt to a more manageable £30 million, United were still urgently in need of fresh investment to stave off the threat of administration.

Before he arrived at Leeds, Garland had duped his next-door neighbour out of £164,000 by claiming to run a company financing transfer deals for top football teams. Garland had claimed his business, Finance for Sport Worldwide, was making so much money that he offered his next-door neighbour Brian Manley, in Strensall, York, a too-good-to-refuse 30-per-cent-return investment. But the 39-year-old confidence trickster, who claimed his firm was involved with Liverpool, Dundee United, Sunderland, Manchester City and Queens Park Rangers, simply used his neighbour's money to buy himself a convertible Porsche 911, a Range Rover and lavish holidays to Florida, Mauritius and a villa in Monaco.

Prosecutor John Edwards said that Garland lured Mr Manley, 50, a printer, and his wife, Philippa, 45, into a bogus investment scheme soon after moving next door to the couple. In January 2001, Mr Manley invested money in Garland's scheme and over the following year the con man had swindled £164,000. Mr Manley said, 'It has just been hell, the worst years of our lives. He was just so callous. He planned it and orchestrated it. He was very charming. We socialised and used to go to the pub with him. We used to treat his children. He came here for meals and we went to his house for a drink. We thought he was genuine.'

Garland offered Mr Manley a 30-per-cent return on his cash, claiming London-based brokers Houlders Insurance – a real firm with no connection to the fraudster – had offered him a high-interest investment opportunity.

'We believed him because we thought he was a genuine guy,' Mr Manley said. 'Chairmen of football clubs believe him. When it comes to con men, he is pretty much up there – he is an artist.

'The alarm bells started ringing because he had just gone out of the country and was really messing us about.'

The couple said they had lost their retirement savings, would have to sell their house to stay afloat financially and could not afford to support their children through university.

'He is just the lowest of the low,' Mr Manley said. 'He just does not care about anybody but himself.'

Judge Paul Hoffman, sentencing Garland to two and a half years, told him, 'What you did was quite despicable. You systematically used friendship to fleece your victims by what I regard as a serious and quite outrageous deception.

'I believe you conned them because you could. You used them as your own private money bank.'

Garland pleaded guilty to 11 charges of obtaining money and property by deception.

Prior to that, in 2004, Garland had been asked by Morris to find people who would help inject cash into Leeds to help get rid of the £30-million debt. Early in September, Garland found what he believed would be an acceptable solution to all concerned. An American company called Nova, based in Tampa, USA, were interested in doing a deal. The plan got as far as writing up a contract and offering it to Nova to sign, but, according to Garland, Simon Morris did not give Nova enough time to complete. Against their wishes, they had to call it off.

The answer to the board's prayers then appeared to be a deal which Garland had brokered with a British–American group led by Sebastian Sainsbury, great-grandson of the founder of the Sainsbury's supermarket chain. By the end of October 2004, they were said to be on the verge of putting pen to paper, after tabling a £25-million offer. Two weeks later, however, the takeover collapsed after the transatlantic consortium failed to come up with the necessary cash. United were forced to sell off their Elland Road home to keep their heads above water – but Garland was not to be deterred.

In late November 2004, he set up another attempt by Sainsbury to seize control of Leeds. This time around, the club's would-be saviour claimed to have secured European backing for his plans – yet, once again, no end product was forthcoming. According to Chris Middleton, Simon Morris was partly to blame for both the Nova and the Sainsbury deals falling through. Middleton alleged that Morris had been asking for bungs: 'I became aware that certain dealings were going on with Sebastian Sainsbury and Nova, and I knew that Simon was trying to take money out of the deal illegally. I couldn't do anything about that. I was an employee. I knew they were demanding deals. Paul Garland got very frustrated that the deals fell through because of greed.'

Sainsbury pulled the plug on the deal in early 2005, paving the way for current chairman Ken Bates's arrival at Leeds eight days later.

Simon Morris continued to deny all the allegations vehemently, whilst seeking legal advice on how to get on top of them. Allegations of plotting to spike a footballer's food with drugs and pay a hit man to end the career of the club's longest-serving player were serious. Morris said, 'Every story is a load of rubbish. None of them [the accusations] is commercially viable – there would be no benefit for Leeds United in doing any of them.

'These are the sort of things kids talk about – it is ridiculous. None of it stacks up. We did not have a replacement for Gary Kelly. It is all nonsense. If he is in hospital for four weeks, it is going to cost £100,000 [in wages].

'And what would have been the benefit of Peter Reid being on Ecstasy? As a board, we did a good job, because the club faced liquidation when we took over . . . We brought in around £40 million in nine months to save the club.'

Turning to the allegations of illegal bungs in connection with Nova Financial Partners and Sebastian Sainsbury, Morris added: 'There were no back-handers.' Morris revealed that blocking a deal would not have been in his or the rest of the board's interests due to a guarantee they had signed on taking over in 2005. He said, 'We had to make a sworn declaration to guarantee the solvency of the business for 12 months. It is done to protect the creditors, and that does not run out until 18 March 2006. If the club proves not to be solvent before then, we face criminal prosecution.

'We had to project cash flows when we took over, and our figures included £8.75 million for the seat debentures. How wrong we were.'

8

Michael Owen: Baby Face

Gangsters? Michael Owen? No chance. Football's squeaky-clean Milky Bar Kid is the last person in the world that adoring fans would expect to be associated with the underworld. But it's true. Even the most boring player on Earth has found himself targeted by vicious criminals wanting to get their hands on his cash or use his prestige for their own despicable ends. One gang even tried to kidnap his sister.

Michael Owen's run-in with some of Britain's biggest drug-dealers is a classic example of how even the unlikeliest of footballers can fall prey to gangsters. One gang of wanted international criminals wheedled their way into the trusting star's inner circle without him knowing, even staying in his hotel rooms before games. Other gangsters sent him death threats for a variety of reasons, ranging from extortion to blaming him for his team's poor performance. And, worst of all, hooded hoodlums tried to force his sister into a car in a kidnap attempt – while she was four months pregnant.

The attack happened on 20 January 2004 when Owen's older sister, Karen, was getting into her car. She had just finished a workout at her local gym, St David's Park Hotel, near her North Wales home, when two hooded men pounced and tried to force her and themselves into her BMW. Violently, the men demanded she drive them away. But the terrified 28-year-old mother-of-one struggled, broke free and was able to raise the alarm. The assailants broke off and ran away. Karen was uninjured but badly shaken following the attack. Her father, Terry, said, 'Karen was threatened with violence. But she raised the alarm and managed to struggle free as the men fled, and some passers-by ran to her aid.'

The kidnap attempt deeply worried security chiefs at Liverpool FC, as well as Owen himself and his very publicity-shy family. What did the men want? Were they going to hold her hostage? Was the attack related to the string of death threats Owen had received over the past couple of years?

Police immediately reviewed security around the family, many of whom live in a cul-de-sac of luxury houses bought for them by multimillionaire Owen. Sergeant Dave Roberts, of North Wales Police, said, 'As she approached her vehicle in the car park, she was approached by two young males who demanded that she drive them somewhere. The female refused and there was a bit of a struggle, and one of the males attempted to grab the keys. The two males did not continue with the struggle and ran away.'

Two months later, Owen spoke for the first time about the death threats that had recently plagued him and other big names in the game, including Liverpool boss Gerard Houllier. Owen said that the sickening phenomenon was a fact of life in modern football. He revealed that not only himself – but none other than England skipper David Beckham – had received over a dozen death threats. Owen was prompted to talk about the dark side of football after Gerard Houllier stunned the world of sport by admitting he had received an anonymous death threat in March 2004. Merseyside Police launched an investigation into the incident, which the respected Anfield chief had not even told his wife about. Owen revealed, 'There are things in football and in life which change, and this is something which has come more into the game. If you speak to David [Beckham], I'm sure he will tell you this kind of thing's happened to him about a dozen times. I've lost count of the amount of times it's happened to me. And it's not just letters. Worse things have occurred.

'Sadly, these days, it seems it can happen to anyone in a high-profile position.

'To be honest, although it is awful, nothing surprises me any more. It should not happen and it is not acceptable, but it is almost part and parcel of the game nowadays. I was as disgusted by the threat on the manager as anyone else. There's no place for that kind of thing in the game or in life. But I know he's handling it. He knows it is just one person and will see it for what it is. You can't let it get to you.

'It's the kind of thing that wouldn't have happened years ago. But it's happening to people regularly now.'

The threat to Houllier was sent on an A4 piece of paper to Anfield, but Houllier opened it at the club's Melwood training ground. Beckham received a number of death threats at his former home in Alderley Edge, Cheshire, when he played for Manchester United. He has revealed that his wife, Victoria, also received chilling letters and in 2003 bought a bulletproof BMW for £150,000 to protect herself. In May 2000, police were called in after Victoria received a specific death threat: a defaced newspaper photograph with a drawing of a bullet pointing towards her. The image was also said to show blood pouring from her head, with the message 'You are going to get what's coming to you'. Earlier that year, a doctored picture of Brooklyn bleeding from a bullet wound to his head was also sent to the home of Beckham's parents.

Owen had been clearly shaken by the new presence of the underworld in the game that he lived and breathed – especially since he had always taken precautions designed specifically to avoid his clean-cut image being tarnished and his lifestyle coming into disrepute. Owen's father, Terry, was a former Everton football player, so he knew the pitfalls of attracting the wrong crowd. He protected his prodigy well. The main advantage Owen had was that he hadn't been brought up in Liverpool.

FOOTBALL AND GANGSTERS

Terry had moved his family out to the quieter pastures of North Wales when he was young, and therefore Owen had none of the natural links other players had to the underworld in a big city. Second, Owen wasn't a big socialiser. Unlike Liverpool's infamous Spice Boys, including self-confessed hell-raisers Robbie Fowler and Steve McManaman, Owen wasn't to be found hanging around the fleshpots of Liverpool's bustling nightlife, where they were at risk of falling into compromising situations. Even when Owen went to private parties, he famously refused to let his guard down. In addition, Owen had a stable family life and had been dating his childhood sweetheart and future wife Louise Bonsall for years. At one party hosted by Robbie Fowler, he stood quietly in a room sipping the same drink all night. Owen's only vice was gambling on the gee-gees, and he could do that safely sat at home in front of the telly, in his huge stately manor, on the phone and over the Internet.

The simple fact was Owen did not seem to have the inclination or the opportunities to want to get to know gangsters. Some footballers loved to hang around with high-profile faces. It boosted their ego. They had a laugh. Apart from anything else, the rootin'-tootin' scallies knew how to enjoy themselves. They had the dough as well to keep up with free-spending footy players. In addition, on a night out with the lads, it was often useful to have a few hard fellas on the firm to deter the drunken idiots from having a go. And if there was anything else required to spice up the party, no doubt they could supply it. For Owen, those kinds of thoughts were blasphemous. His temperament was too even-keel. At the end of the day, many Liverpool fans were grateful that he was a sensible woollyback who loved playing golf and did not allow good times to interfere with his form.

However, even with a full range of personal and familial security measures in place, Owen astonishingly became a victim. In the late '90s, the player became pals with one of Britain's most wanted drug-barons. Several other England and Liverpool stars also formed a worrying friendship with the fugitive villain and members of his

128

very dangerous gang. Gangland underboss Tom Foley, then 36, had just jumped bail on drug-dealing charges when he became very close pals with Owen and his teammates. In addition, several other Liverpool underworld faces frequently socialised with the stars in the exclusive players' lounge at the Anfield ground and in hotels after away games.

While police from two forces had been hunting the fugitive for two years, Foley and his shady pals had been living it up with Owen, Robbie Fowler, Paul Ince, Steve McManaman and Jamie Carragher. The footballers got so close to Foley and his gang that they allowed them right into Owen and Carragher's hotel bedroom for photos – even when they were still in bed! The stars posed on several occasions for pictures with fugitive Foley at exclusive, invitation-only post-match parties.

None of the stars were aware of the criminal background of Foley and his friends – or that Foley is an associate of Britain's wealthiest drug king, Curtis Warren. Merseyside Police were keen to speak to the players to see if they could help trace Foley. Fans were shocked that some of soccer's brightest young guns were socialising with Liverpool's underworld. A source at Liverpool FC said at the time, 'This is a massive blow to the image of the club. These footballers are regarded as the cream of the crop, and yet they have been mixing with men like these. There will have to be a full investigation into how this was allowed to happen at a club that promotes a family atmosphere.'

Foley – dubbed the Scarlet Pimpernel by the Liverpool underworld because of his ability to evade capture and for his life-long support for red-shirted Liverpool – had been on the run since July 1998. A warrant for his arrest was issued after he failed to turn up for his trial at Preston Crown Court in Lancashire on charges of supplying heroin and cannabis. But within a month, Foley and convicted hoodlum Michael Murphy – who also grew up with the notorious Curtis Warren and has convictions for malicious wounding, robbery, burglary and car theft – were rubbing shoulders with the England and Arsenal goalkeeper David Seaman after a Liverpool v. Arsenal match. Seaman had no idea of the background of his new acquaintances.

But Foley was able to infiltrate Liverpool's inner circle because he had struck up a friendship with one of the players at the pub where they both drank: The Chaucer, in the Bootle area of Merseyside. For two years, between 1998 and 2000, Foley and his dodgy chums boozed with the club's most respected stars at the team hotel following Premiership matches in cities like Newcastle and Southampton. They got so close that one of Foley's mates, Martin Foster, was photographed with Owen and Carragher in the players' bedroom. Again, both players were still in bed. At the time, Foster was facing trial for possession of 27 kg of heroin.

But the most astonishing sign of how close Foley had come to Owen and the team came on 30 August 1998 when Liverpool were playing a crunch Premiership game against Newcastle United. The star striker scored a sensational goal and was then clearly seen gleefully rubbing his hands together in a bizarre post-goal celebration, which was screened on BBC's *Match of the Day*. Owen's curious manner was exactly the same as Foley's. A Liverpool gangland source told us: 'When Foley gets excited about something or is pleased with himself, he always rubs his hands together. Owen, Jamie Carragher and the other Liverpool lads think it's hilarious the way Tom does it and started to mimic him.'

Foley was so popular he was given match tickets to Liverpool home games. He was treated as a VIP, with much-sought-after passes to after-game get-togethers in the players' lounge. The gangland source added: 'It's very difficult to get passes for the players' lounge – they really are like gold dust. But Foley never had a problem.'

Foley's mate Michael Murphy refused to discuss their association with the stars when we questioned him. A former pal of Foley's said, 'People like Michael Owen ought to be more careful about who they mix with. These rogues are just using the footballers for their own purposes.'

In 2001, Foley was remanded in custody by magistrates on drugs charges from which he had been on the run for over two and a half years. Foley had finally been arrested after a painstaking police operation in Aberdeen.

9

Robbie Fowler: the £28-Million Man

Premiership veteran Robbie Fowler has been plagued by the underworld for many years. Gangsters blackmailed the Liverpool returnee over his sister's addiction to drugs. A masked tie-up gang raided his house when he was at Leeds, intending to hold him or his family hostage in a bid to get him to hand over cash and valuables. Evil underworld bosses also mounted a vicious smear campaign accusing him of taking drugs in another attempt to force him to hand over money. In addition, completely unknown to Fowler, the lawyer who took over managing his affairs was bent. And, finally, a notorious hard-man appointed himself as a minder to Robbie in a bid to ingratiate himself with the multimillionaire star.

Fowler could have been one of England's legends – predatory, instinctive, deadly in the box. But mystery has always surrounded why he never realised his full potential. Of course, he has had a great career, amassing an estimated £28-million fortune along the way, making him Britain's fourth-richest player, according to the *Sunday Times Rich List*. He has had a first-team place at several of the great clubs and has returned to one of the biggest and best to play out his final days. Some achievement. But some pundits have accused him of settling for less in the ambition stakes, of drifting from club to club like a journeyman rather than a king. Other commentators have said that Fowler has never truly reached the toppermost of his profession, criticising him for lacking the mental focus and lifestyle discipline to become a truly magnificent athlete. Injury prevented him from playing in the England squad for the 1998 World Cup. Rather than ask 'Where did it all go wrong?', many diehard fans have always asked 'Why didn't it all go right?', bearing in mind the incredible football hand he was dealt to begin with.

Some journalists have agreed that the menace of the underworld, which has always been in the background of Fowler's life, could have played a part in putting him off balance from time to time during his career. Once again, his story follows the familiar pattern of the working-class boy wonder come good who is unable to escape the smell of the street, who cannot, despite his best intentions, shake off the bad influences that formed part of his childhood environment.

Fowler was raised in the Park Road area of Liverpool's tough dockside districts, Dingle and Toxteth. Not only were these neighbourhoods hard, but they were heavily influenced, if not controlled, by highly organised crime gangs. Most of the mobs, who were built around close familial or ethnic ties, started off as thieves systematically plundering the eight and a half miles of Liverpool docks that had made the city legitimately rich during the days of empire. When the containerised and highly mechanised Port of Liverpool took over from the old docks in the '70s and '80s, the gangs graduated into other forms of trade-based crime, such as contraband-smuggling and then on to drug-dealing – the crime which would make them rich beyond their wildest dreams. Park Road, the street in which Robbie Fowler had spent much of his early years, became the hub of a huge international drugs network stretching from Turkey to Colombia to Japan.

Fowler burst onto the Premiership stage in 1993 when he scored five goals in his Anfield debut in a Coca-Cola Cup match against Fulham. He quickly notched up domestic honours, including the Coca-Cola Cup in 1995 and two PFA Young Player of the Year awards in 1995 and 1996. He went on to dazzle Liverpool and England fans with his goal-scoring ability, an entertaining combination of quick-footed ball control and scallywag guile which outwitted opponents time and again. These were his glory years, played out to a soundtrack of The Farm, Happy Mondays and Cream dance-music compilations.

As Robbie held court at Anfield stadium in the north of the city, the gangs in the southern districts of his birthplace were also getting busy. Coincidentally, the 1990s were the golden age of drug-dealing, brought on by an unprecedented period of year-on-year narco super-growth arising from a winning combination of market advantages, such as industrial farming of drug crops, cheap international travel, the explosion of communications technology and financial deregulation. At the same time that Robbie was putting them in for the Reds, lads who had grown up just streets away from him were having an equally big impact on their chosen world, scoring huge amounts of drugs on the international market and shipping them back to the UK. For instance, Toxteth-born Curtis Warren was importing cocaine in 1,000-kilo loads direct from Colombia. The trade netted him a cool £200 million. Coincidentally again, Warren had exactly the same investment plan as Fowler – they both put their money almost wholesale into property, buying up entire streets of terraced houses all over Britain. Warren became the richest criminal in Britain; Fowler the richest footballer (though, of course, the two were never connected).

Two notorious families dominated Fowler's boyhood manor. The Ungi and the Fitzgibbon clans were both feared and respected. They had national and international links. In 1995, businessman and well-known 'community leader' David Ungi, the head of the family, was killed in a hail of automatic gunfire as he cruised the streets in which Fowler had mastered his knockabout skills. The pub that the families used as their base, the infamous 'Black' George's, was so close to Robbie's family home that he often went there for a pint.

The unfailingly polite, quietly spoken Fowler also used to frequent the run-down betting shop on the corner over the road. He went in to place his own bets and also to put on wagers for his ageing grandfather if he couldn't get there himself. To get to the bulletproof counter, next to the steel-plated office door, Fowler had to weave through the islands of smoke-engulfed punters who stood dead-eyed watching the dog races on the iron-reinforced, anti-theft telly or the results scrawled up with watery markers on the colour-coded magi-board. A bet-settler working inside the shop said, 'Robbie is very shy. You'd only have to let on to him and say "All right, Robbie" and he'd go red.

'He started coming in when he was 16, before he hit the big-time and was playing for one of the Liverpool lower teams. I remember him buying his first car. It was quite an old one, and one night when I was locking up I shouted over, messing about: "This time next year, it'll be a Ferrari."

'He said, "I wish."

'Of course, it came true. The next year, he broke into the first team, and the rest is history.'

Many of the punters he swerved through on the way to the Formica betting counter were international drug-barons with plastic bags full of betting cash under their arms or bundles of notes stuffed inside their £400-a-time one-off Italian trackies. The odd one, knowing him from around the barrio and that he deserved respect as an up-and-coming footballer, let on almost imperceptibly – the slightest movement of a sly eye. For a villain, even that was the equivalent of kissing arse in poker-faced gangster land. The half-let-on was a measure of the respect 'our Robbie' was held in.

It was from this culture that Robbie had to break free. I first noticed how the player had unknowingly become entangled in the city's underworld when the *Sunday Mirror* assigned me to do a story about him in the late '90s. The tip was that Robbie was about to get married to his fiancée – nothing too scandalous, but a half-decent story for a tabloid, bearing in mind that Robbie, the Spice Boy hell-raiser of one of Britain's top glamour clubs, was finally settling down.

His partner in rock and roll was fellow Spice Boy McManaman – he was managed by Spice Girls guru Simon Fuller and hung out with a group of fashionable young footballing stars such as Jamie Redknapp. The Spice Boys have been dogged by accusations that they were too fond of partying. McManaman and Fowler gave a raunchy 'birds, booze and BMWs' interview to *Loaded* in 1995, and it has been used to give them a hard time ever since. This is in spite of Fowler's claims that their answers were jokey blokey ones and not intended for publication. Fowler specifically says that when the interviewer left the room to go to the toilet, he and mischievous Macca picked up a written list of questions and playfully delivered a load of far-fetched, over-the-top answers, without realising that the tape was still running. When the journalist played back the tape later, he used these answers, rather than the more boring on-the-record ones which followed.

On the ground in Liverpool, I started crunching gravel, knocking on the doors of Robbie's friends and family in an attempt to get some quotes to stand up the story. Within about half an hour, I got a call on my mobile from Robbie's personal legal eagle, none other than local-lad-made-good and solicitor to the stars Kevin Dooley. In typical over-the-top style, the dramatic Dooley began to threaten me. He said, 'If you don't stop harassing my client, I will take action.'

'I'm not harassing your client,' I replied.

'If you go within 30 yards of my client's house again, I will get a restraining order against you.'

'It's not unlawful to knock at someone's door,' I reminded him.

'If you don't leave my client alone, then you are going to regret it.'

Politely, I informed Dooley that if he had any further problems, he should address them directly to the Mirrror Group lawyers at Canary Wharf in London. I had skin like a crocodile and was used to being given a hard time while doing stories, so it was no big deal.

Dooley's bully-boy tactics were notorious on the legal circuit in Merseyside. Dooley not only represented sports stars such as Kenny Dalglish, Graeme Souness and Everton striker Duncan Ferguson, but, unbeknown to them, he also acted for several high-profile gangsters, such as drug supremo Curtis Warren. Like many underworld hangers-on, he had begun to adopt some of their ways. His gangster-like behaviour had led to him being dubbed Alfonso by members of the Liverpool mafia, who viewed his penchant for pin-striped suits and thick-cuffed shirts, and his histrionic threats to those who crossed him, with bemusement. One Liverpool godfather, who has made tens of millions of pounds from extortion, enforcing and drug-dealing, said, 'One time, someone upset him over something or other and Alfonso said, "He's going to be sleeping with the fishes." I actually heard him say that. I couldn't believe it. He actually thought he was in the Mafia.'

In retaining Dooley as a lawyer, Fowler had unwittingly chosen a corrupt solicitor who, at the same time as representing him, was engaged in fraudulent get-rich-quick schemes for which he would later be struck off. Mr Dooley was warned by his own bank manager that certain of his transactions might be fraudulent in October 1996. Despite this warning, his career was to end in shame further down the line, after allegations of impropriety forced his firm to close. He had been accused of working with a suspected criminal in high-yield investments between 1995 and 2000. A tribunal was told that 19 phoney investments promised returns of 1,400 per cent and bore all the hallmarks of a bank investment fraud.

This was not the only controversy that would blight Dooley's career before it finally ended, though. In 2002, he was at the centre of a corruption probe at Liverpool Magistrates' Court which also implicated two judges and four senior clerks. He was alleged to have received favourable treatment in exchange for gifts and football tickets. All were cleared after a police investigation and an internal inquiry. However, Dooley was eventually struck off following the unconnected Law Society investigation into his financial affairs. Fellow solicitors disliked his way of operating. Liverpool solicitor Rex Makin said, 'He caused terrible trouble for the legal profession. It was absolutely dreadful. As a fellow advocate, I thought his advocacy skills were useless, yet he attracted such big names.'

None of Dooley's bad behaviour had come to light at the time I was running around Liverpool trying to find out whether Fowler was eventually going to tie the knot. Dooley was still a name to be reckoned with. So, an hour after his abusive rant, I received a panicky call from a *Sunday Mirror* lawyer asking me to tread carefully. Perhaps the lawyer in his Canary Wharf office was not used to Dooley's street tactics and was afraid to stand up to his reputation. I continued to make enquiries. That night, I jumped on a train back to London, and just as we were pulling out of Lime Street Station my mobile went off.

The man on the other end introduced himself as Jay-Jay Calf. He was a medium-tier drug-dealer from Park Road, Robbie Fowler's old neighbourhood. Jay-Jay could often be seen standing in the betting shop frequented by Fowler, with a small blue pen in the side of his mouth, a yellow and white betting slip in one hand and a plastic bag containing approximately £30,000 stuffed into the front of his sagging designer tracksuit. Every few minutes, he would put his hand inside, pull out a bundle of notes and instruct the cashier to write a bet out. 'A hundred to win. Trap two, girl.' 'Five hundred double, trap six in the three-fifteen at such and such, and trap four in the three-thirty.' Often, thousands of pounds of drug profits would go back and forth. Jay-Jay often parked his two cars – one an RS Cosworth, which was popular at the time – outside the shop unlocked, in an area where robbing had been elevated to an art form. His car was never stolen. In short, Jay-Jay was a respected and well-known 'community leader' – a gangster.

Jay-Jay had been set upon me by Dooley without the knowledge or permission of Fowler. Jay-Jay was media-wise. He and his brother had infamously been bodyguards to a very high-profile TV comedian in the early '80s. The unfortunate entertainer didn't know they were gangsters. Unscrupulously, the gangsters set up the celebrity with prostitutes and then turned him over for the *News of the World*. On another occasion, he had once threatened a *Sunday Mirror* reporter while he was investigating a corruption scandal involving his pal. He had warned the fleeing reporter, 'I'm going to send you back to London in a body-bag.'

In his warning to me, Jay-Jay's air was menacing. He said, 'Robbie is a mate of ours. I know that you're looking into him. If you don't stop, then I will deal with you. If you ever knock on his door, then I'll knock on yours.'

An underworld source later told me, 'Jay-Jay had nothing to do with Robbie. But he did have connections to Dooley. Dooley tipped him off. Jay-Jay appointed himself as Robbie's minder. It's like a protection racket – after they scared off the reporters, Jay-Jay thought it would curry favour with Robbie. And then they could start tapping him for money to protect him in the future. It's basically taxing.'

In the mid-'90s, Fowler was dragged into another underworld drama. He began paying blackmail money to a drugs gang, handing over hundreds of pounds in a desperate bid to stop the blackmailers exposing the drug problems of his sister Lisa. He was approached by the gang – allegedly one of the crime clans from his Dingle neighbourhood with connections to gangsters like Jay-Jay – at his £300,000 mansion and told, 'Cough up or we go public on what we know about Lisa.' They told him they knew that Lisa had been having problems with drugs and that she had been attending a dependency unit. Robbie had taken his troubled sister to live with him as she battled to overcome her habit. And she was well on her way to beating the addiction when the blackmailers turned up.

A friend of Fowler's at the time said, 'Robbie and his family were horrified. Lisa had only just beaten her drug habit and was still at a very delicate stage. They were desperately worried that any kind of publicity would send her over the edge again. Lisa adores Robbie, and the last thing she would want to do is harm him or his career. It would have plunged her into total despair. She was always anxious not to drag Robbie's name into her drugs mess.'

To protect his sister, Fowler ordered cash payments to be made through an intermediary to the blackmailers. It is understood that bundles of cash in used notes were paid to shadowy figures over several months. But eventually the strain became so great that the family decided to call in the police. Fowler also informed his club bosses at Liverpool. The friend said, 'Robbie had thought the blackmailers would eventually go away. But, if anything, their demands increased. The strain on Robbie was tremendous.

'He had done everything humanly possible to help Lisa, and now he was landed with this. Robbie became quiet and withdrawn, a far cry from his usual self. In the end, he thought he had no alternative but to go to the police.'

Despite an investigation, no one was ever charged. In his excellent book *Fowler: My Autobiography*, co-written by *Mirror* sports journalist David Maddock, Robbie recalls how the police tried to sting the blackmailers:

> We went to the police right away. They got Lisa to organise a meeting with the blackmailers, and then she was wired up just like the movies. It was pretty exciting, actually. So she then went along with this electronic stuff on her, and with all the police tailing her and listening in, and we were all holding our breath, wondering what would happen. But the fuckers never turned up.

Lisa, then 23, had fallen into the clutches of drug-barons as a teenager growing up. According to family friends, she was 'always desperate for money' to feed her habit. Eventually, she received counselling for drug dependency at Liverpool's Maryland Centre. She moved into the five-bedroom house bought by Fowler in Liverpool where he'd lived with his mum, Marie, and his brothers before setting up a home with his wife. His dad, Robbie Senior, was separated from his mum.

In revenge for reporting them to the police, the blackmailers then targeted Fowler himself. They launched a long-running smear campaign trying to link Fowler with drugs himself, in the hope of getting him to pay them off.

Fowler's anguish began with a letter through his front door. It spelled out a threat in the most chilling terms possible: 'Give us the cash or we'll tell the world we've seen you snorting cocaine.' More poison-pen notes, full of the same false accusations, continued to arrive, driving the shattered striker to the brink of despair. Fowler took a close friend into his confidence to tell him about the outrageous lies: 'The stories are being spread by people who are jealous of me. Do you think I'd risk my career, my livelihood, by taking drugs when I know the FA's testing unit are turning up unannounced at our training ground almost every week?'

Though Fowler was the darling of the Kop and earlier that season was reported to have demanded a new £50,000-a-week contract, he felt his life was being ruined by the rumours. He added to a friend, 'Even though the stories are so obviously lies, they are hurting my family. My parents and my sister are hearing that I'm supposed to be wandering around like a zombie, drugged to the eyeballs. They don't believe it, of course, but it still upsets them, and I find that difficult to deal with.'

Fowler handled the latest accusations in the same way as he had handled the case involving his sister – by going straight to club officials. He told them what was going on and showed them the blackmail notes. But Fowler was still finding it hard to cope with the pressure, which some people said accounted for a loss of form during the 1998 season. He had been going through one of the leanest spells in his career so far. At about the same time as the drug blackmail letters, he was dropped by the England coach Glenn Hoddle, effectively ending his hopes of an appearance in World Cup '98 in France. Teammate Michael Owen, then just 18, took over his national role in a friendly against Chile as the youngest England player of the last century.

As crisis loomed, Fowler admitted, 'I haven't been at my best, it's true. But I'll never hide, even if I'm not playing brilliantly. If I miss a goal, then I'll keep my head up, confident that I'll put the next one away.'

Fowler revealed how widespread the smear stories were becoming. He said, 'One of my friends got into a cab in Liverpool and the driver started telling him how he'd seen me snorting cocaine on the back seat. My friend never told the driver he knew me and the story was untrue, but he told me because he thought I ought to be aware. If a cabbie says things like that about me, who else is spreading this rubbish? I've even had people asking me personally if it's true I take drugs. When it first happened, it was a bit of a joke, but now it's become so frustrating. I know the rumours are that I'm not playing well because I'm a drug-addict, but it's simply not true. Everyone at Liverpool knows it's rubbish. All the players, not only me, have been tested for drugs much more recently. If I took anything, I'd be caught straight away.

'I would be daft if I tried anything. My manager Roy Evans would boot me out of Liverpool and my career would be over.

'People have to understand this is the way I earn my living. I'd lose everything if I was that stupid. But these people sending me these blackmail threats are ruining my life. I don't need all this hassle.

'I just want to concentrate on playing football, but it's hard when you've got these people on your back all the time.'

Fowler's friend recalled how the England star told him he had been targeted by drug-dealers. According to the friend, Fowler told him, 'People know you are a footballer and have got money. They think you are going to spend it on drugs. But it's wrong, and I don't want to know. I've never touched drugs.'

But the rumours persisted, not helped by that infamous interview for *Loaded* magazine in which Fowler and fellow Liverpool player Steve McManaman had revelled in their footy-blingy lifestyle and boasted how they liked to go clubbing and late-night gambling and all the rest of it. McManaman told how Fowler had borrowed £100 from him so he could have a bet in a Liverpool bookies. McManaman said, 'There you go. Put a hundred quid on a horse you've never seen or even heard of. It's a mug's game.' McManaman also revealed how he and Fowler enjoyed spending their surplus cash at casinos. He said, 'We only ever spend a short time in there. We get bored. We end up putting all our money on red or something – nine hundred quid on one number or something.'

Fowler had scored more than thirty goals in each of the three seasons between 1994 and 1997. His skill has brought him the reward of seven England caps, scoring twice for his country. But during the 1997–98 season, his form seemed to leave him dramatically, and he scored just 13 goals.

FOOTBALL AND GANGSTERS

The following year, Fowler was taken to task for pretending to snort the white line of the Anfield penalty area after scoring in a Merseyside derby. It was meant to be an act of defiance in the face of an antagonistic local crowd determined to slate him over the drug rumours. But the gesture simply deepened the hole he was in. He was suspended for the final games of the season after the cocaine-sniffing joke and fined a staggering £32,000 by his own club.

In a PR damage-limitation exercise, the troubled star opened his heart to millions of TV viewers in an interview with big-name confessor Martin Bashir, in the hope that people would understand the motives behind the ill-judged goal celebration. He referred to an unnamed 'family member' who had become embroiled in drugs – obviously his older sister Lisa. Fowler told Bashir he'd never been lured by drugs, despite persistent rumours and his controversial white-line-sniffing joke. He said he could never have become a drug-user after seeing the hell a relative had gone through: 'I've had family members who've been into drugs. I can see what it does to them and I'm not stupid enough to be like one of them. Obviously, you are just going to try to help them as best you can.'

A close family friend added: 'Robbie has done everything in his power to get Lisa back on her feet. He didn't name her, because he's always been careful not to expose his family to the same spotlight he lives in. She is doing really well now and he doesn't want to do anything that might tip her over the edge.'

But, despite his efforts, Fowler could not leave his scallywag past behind him. He still frequented the city-centre Moat House hotel – now closed down, but in its heyday a magnet for gangsters far and wide. Tommy 'Tacker' Comerford, identified by Customs and Excise as Britain's first heroin-baron, used the hotel when it was a Holiday Inn in the '80s as a base for his cocaine ring.

During the 1990s, I used to stay there on newspaper assignments. The bar past the reception area often looked like a drug-dealers' convention, as gangsters and doormen held meetings to discuss graft. At one time, it was the official Liverpool FC pre-match hotel. A lot of dark secrets were never allowed to leave the premises, held prisoner by the super-discreet staff. I had witnessed a lot of behaviour there. I'd watched the girlfriend of a young Everton star bleed over the polished marble floor after he'd beaten her up. I had sat in a room as a drunk Robbie Fowler lay on a bed surrounded by adoring girls – a few days before his England debut.

The atmosphere in there could be harsh. I remember a load of gangsters humiliating a man for looking like Noel Gallagher as he waited for the lift to join a Robbie Fowler party. The 20-strong gang – all high on cocaine – abused the poor reveller for wanting to 'kiss Robbie's arse'. They were only finally thrown out of the hotel in the early hours after the arrival of two vanloads of riot police who had been called to stop a mass brawl in the reception area.

It was in this place that Fowler chose to socialise. It was only a matter of time before it came ontop. It soon did. One night, Fowler was beaten up in the toilets. Twenty-four-year-old Paul Noon admitted punching the player and was later convicted of unlawful and malicious wounding. He was jailed for 18 months after a court heard how Fowler suffered a broken nose, a chipped tooth, a black eye and bruising to the back of his head.

10

The Footy Player, the Rap Star and the Gangster

An evil gangster threatened to kidnap the wife and newborn baby of Portsmouth midfielder Sean Davis if he didn't hand over £30,000, according to sources close to the footballer. The hard-tackling former Tottenham star was playing an away match when the villain knocked on the door of his luxury London house and demanded the cash, or else, while the baby slept upstairs. When Davis found out, he was terrified and at a loss as to what to do. He knew that if he called in the police, it might antagonise the kidnapper even more. If he paid up, that would mean the beginning of the end. Who could he turn to?

The most astonishing fact about the Sean Davis drama is that the kidnapper – whom we'll call Sid (not his real name) – was an old childhood associate of the player. Sid had grown up in the tough streets of Lambeth with Davis. Whereas Davis had gone on to a bright future, signing up for Fulham's youth academy as a teenager, Asian-born Sid had taken a different route. He grew into a violent underworld debt-collector and extortionist. But when a criminal deal went wrong, Sid ended up owing tens of thousands of pounds to godfathers all over London.

In desperation, he hit on the idea of taxing wealthy people he knew around his manor. Even in the council estates and the suburbs of south London, there was enough blingy celebrity wealth to keep a taxman busy. First, he turned on a very famous south London rapper turned TV star, a popular singer–frontman of a top-selling urban act, who was a friend of Sean Davis's. He began making threats against the rap star. On at least one occasion, he phoned an associate of the star's and said to pass the message on that he would shoot him. The rapper was having none of it and managed to fend off Sid. He was no shrinking violet.

In May 2005, the rapper was sentenced to 150 hours of community service for violently attacking a police officer the previous January. At St Albans Magistrates' Court, he was found guilty of assaulting Constable Keith Harron and using threatening behaviour. The 27 year old had been given a tug for illegally using a mobile phone while driving his Volkswagen car, but he allegedly ripped off Harron's tie as he tried to arrest him in Welwyn, Hertfordshire. Officers were forced to blast CS spray into the rapper's eyes to end the scuffle.

Added to this lack of fear for authority or reputations, the rapper had the backing of the numerous members of the tough-talking band he belonged to and the homeboys from the Battersea estate where he grew up. In short, the rapper was no pushover and he wasn't going to roll over easily, no matter how much Sid threatened him.

Sean Davis, on the other hand, was an easy target. He was a family man, whose long-term partner Dionne and new baby meant everything to him. He had less backup and he was a cash-rich Premiership player who might want to pay up rather than risk all and cause a fuss. In addition, the squeaky-clean player was at a critical phase in his career, when the pressure of such a horrific ordeal may have tipped him over the edge. Up to that point, he had enjoyed a steady and successful time in the top flight. He was a product of the Craven Cottage youth system and was described by former Fulham and England boss Kevin Keegan as being 'as good as anyone I've seen at his age'. He made his first-team debut aged just 17 years and 25 days. A strong-tackling, solid midfielder who could pass and keep the ball with a maturity well beyond his years,

Sean progressed even further under the guidance of Jean Tigana and Christian Damiano and became a first-team regular. After an exciting 2002–03 campaign in which he firmly established his position in the starting line-up, Davis was finally called up to be part of the England squad that faced Australia.

In November 2004, the rapper spoke about his own and Sean's ordeal at the hands of Sid. He told a friend, 'Obviously, you know Sean. Well, Sid threatened to kidnap Dionne if Sean didn't pay him thirty grand. He went round to his house when Sean was away with Fulham and threatened Dionne. She was scared.

'He threatened my best friend [Sean Davis] . . . for thirty K. He threatened Sean's girlfriend when she was by herself. He went round there and scared the shit out of her. And he threatened me down the phone.'

Davis's head was wrecked. He turned to various people for advice, but it was only when word of his ordeal reached a well-respected face in London that the problem stopped. Without Davis's knowledge, the face had a word with Sid and mediated a peaceful solution to the problem.

A football agent was also privy to the ordeal. He said, 'What he done to Sean, he done, but that is not the true Sid we know. Because he was in need of the money, he went to Sean, innit? But he went about it in the wrong way.

'That is Sid wanting to be the big gangster. It was a bit out of order going to shake up Dionne and considering she had the baby there as well. Sid should have thought more.

'Because this big London mobster was tipped off, he never had to give any money over, ever. Sean's lucky.'

Another source said, 'Sid got into trouble over money. It was crazy that when this gangster spoke to him, he backed off.'

The ordeal shook Davis up, and soon he was looking for another club. By that time, he had played over 100 games for the Cottagers and seemed to be seeking a move away from London. He attracted interest from Everton during that season, and they made a couple of unsuccessful bids for him. Davis then handed in a transfer request citing his ambition to further his career. Middlesbrough joined the race for the young man's signature, with the club saying they would only let the interested parties talk to the player when they had found a suitable replacement. This transfer saga rumbled on for most of the summer, and the striker looked to be heading for Merseyside, until David Moyes pulled out of the deal when he realised the player would not pass a medical before the August transfer deadline because of a knee injury. Davis went on to have one of his best seasons ever, working his way back into the team around November 2003 and scoring six goals from midfield in thirty appearances, before deciding on a move north of the river to Tottenham Hotspur. His first season there, however, was not as successful. After he suffered a knee injury in November, he did not play again until mid-March. All in all, he made only 16 appearances.

Davis always feared Sid would strike again, but fortunately the latter was charged with violence offences and later jailed for four years in connection with a separate case. Sean Davis was free to get on with his life. In January 2006, he left Spurs and the big bad city to join Portsmouth.

11

Extortion Epidemic: the Case Studies

Blackmail and extortion of Britain's biggest players has continued unabated. As recently as February 2006, an evil plot targeting one of the UK's top internationals was smashed. The villain behind the scam, who claimed he had pictures of a Merseyside footballer taking drugs and associating with prostitutes, was sent to jail. Steven Blower, 38, plotted to exchange videotapes and photographs – which did not exist – for £48,000, Liverpool Crown Court heard. He admitted attempting to obtain the cash from a friend of the international and Premiership player's. The court heard he made up the 'malicious and false allegation' for his own financial gain and the footballer was left very concerned and worried by his demands for money.

His MO was textbook taxing, and many players all around the UK will recognise the chilling hallmarks. Prosecutor Nicholas Johnson said Scouser Blower claimed to have a video and photographs showing the footballer with prostitutes and taking cocaine. He said Blower demanded money on a number of occasions between August and October 2005 and even visited the footballer's home. After arranging a meeting with the footballer's friend, Blower claimed he was acting on behalf of a third party, whom he referred to as 'Robbo', who was trying to sell the pictures to a national newspaper. Mr Johnson said, 'Mr Blower said the video was so devastating that even O.J. Simpson's and Michael Jackson's attorney would not be able to help the footballer if it got into the public domain.' Blower claimed a Sunday newspaper had bid £150,000 for the images but offered to hand them over to the footballer for a lesser price. Mr Johnson added: 'Although he wanted the money, he said he did not want the information made public because of the effect on the footballer's career.' He said that Blower arranged a series of clandestine meetings with the footballer's friend – 'conducted like something out of a spy film' – but it backfired when the footballer and his associate informed the police of the blackmail plot.

As Blower arrived at a meeting on 5 October 2005 last year to pick up the blackmail money from the footballer's friend, he was arrested by waiting detectives. Later, he pleaded guilty to blackmail and, jailing him for three and a half years, Judge Henry Globe told the court, 'Those in public life are susceptible to this type of behaviour.'

In another case, a Welsh international footballer was not so lucky. The compromising evidence the blackmailers had on him was real. And when he didn't play the game, he was beaten up and his legs were slashed with a knife. The hell-raising star was one of the game's hard-men, in the style of Graeme Souness and Vinnie Jones. But off the pitch, his image counted for nothing, and when he tried to mix it with some very bad fellows, he crumbled quickly and his life was ruined.

To make things worse, he started living a secret double life, which left him wide open to blackmail. After he tied the knot with his first wife in a registry office in 1985, he maintained to the outside world that he was a happily married family man. But when darkness fell, the player made the mistake of socialising in nightclubs with gangsters and frequenting pubs in a rough area of the city he played in for after-hours drinking sessions. He said, 'Over four of those seven years I was married, I went with lots of women. I couldn't begin to put a number on it. Some of the players used to go down to one particular nightclub and pull a bird. We'd take them to the Holiday Inn and do the business. We were regulars there.'

One of his conquests was unfortunately the wife of a gangster. At first, he was simply warned off by kind pals of the villain, who did not want to see the player get into trouble. But when he cockily ignored the advice and persisted, he was threatened in no uncertain terms. However, the arrogant star continued to try his luck. Consequently, he was beaten up several times. Then, finally, the tops and calves of his legs were slashed in a vicious gangland attack. The assailants tried to stab him in the backside. Afterwards, to make amends, the footballer was forced to hand over thousands of pounds in tribute to the gang boss to prevent further retribution. The player was so terrified he slept with a knife under his bed. He was forced to leave the city with his career and marriage in ruins. The ordeal had a massive psychological effect on the player. He drifted through four top clubs but never regained his form. He soon became depressed and started using cocaine heavily. His second marriage was soon on the rocks through alcoholism. To clean up, he left the country to play abroad.

A former Irish international and Premiership star was taxed by the same vicious gangster family who had once planned to blackmail Steven Gerrard. The Irish player was one of the first cases of taxing in its modern form, and his nightmare scenario had all the characteristics of a classic set-up. The story goes like this: the Ireland star was partying in a very famous nightclub in the mid-'90s. He then became involved in an argument with a young woman, who onlookers claim was behaving deliberately provocatively and may have been a plant by gangster pals of the doormen. Fuelled by too much drink, the usually polite player made several very insulting remarks to her. Several days later, he was contacted by the gangsters, who told him that the girl was 'part of our family'. Without pausing for breath, the menacing voice continued: 'An apology is in order and damages of £10,000 in cash.'

The player was so terrified that he feared to go into the city centre for six months. He confided in the lead singer of a well-known '90s pop group. In the VIP players' lounge at Leeds, the singer then invited the player out for a post-match drink when they returned to their home city later that night, following the away game at Elland Road. The star replied, 'I'd love to but I can't go out in town at the moment. If I do, it will cost me £10,000.

'The gangsters have told me that if I go into town, it will cost me £10,000. And if I haven't got the money, they will me beat me up or worse.'

Consequently, he didn't go for a drink that night. Eventually, the gangsters started making threats to the player directly. When his form began to buckle under the pressure, the Irish international was forced to confide in a member of the security people who guard the national team. Word eventually reached some very heavyweight Dublin-based 'community leaders' who knew the Mr Bigs on the mainland behind the player's heartache. The story goes that the Irish gangsters had a word with their British counterparts and the threats stopped – without money being handed over.

The next case is equally concerning. When Danny X began to make a name for himself at a top Premiership club, he also began to attract the wrong kind of attention. He was befriended by a well-known drug-dealer who began turning up at his suburban mansion offering to give him a lift to training, which was several miles away. Danny X was flattered by the attention of this infamous villain and naively thought that having a gangster 'on the firm' was a status symbol. It was no secret that players at this club often boasted about their shady associates in the dressing-room, where it was bizarrely considered one of the trappings of Premiership wealth and fame. Danny X later told pals that he allowed the drug-dealer to get close to him because he thought, 'Other players have their gangsters, why can't I?' He also revealed that several players regularly got lifts from gangsters to the club's hallowed training ground, using the pretence of 'security reasons' but secretly relishing the gangster chic.

One morning, as Danny X was about to leave the home he shared with his beautiful and also famous girlfriend for training, the gangster pulled up in a brand-new four-by-four outside. He invited him to hop in and said he would drive him to the ground. The following day, the gangster turned up again. During the 30-minute drive, the gangster suddenly asked Danny X if he could borrow £500 in cash. Before he had time to think, the gangster had pulled up next to a cashpoint and was urging the confused player to do him a favour. A couple of days later, the exact same thing happened, but for £200. This went on for many months, pushing Danny X to despair – and his monthly expenses up by several thousand pounds. Danny X was too scared to confront his taxer and too embarrassed to seek help. He was finally rescued from his predicament by modern-day gangland cavalry in the form of a security firm who had declared war on the poor player's terroriser in an unrelated feud, to get control of local nightclubs. One night, they ambushed the gangster in a pub.

After the fray, they found a shaking bystander cowering behind the bar. It was Danny X. He told them how the gangster had taken to stalking him and taxing him at every turn. He told his rescuers, 'He's even started turning up after training to take me home. On the way back, he makes me stop off in the pub, which I don't want to do.' The security firm told the star that he need never worry again. The star was one of the first players to speak out sympathetically against the horrifying influences in the modern game when one of his team colleagues received death threats. He knew the feeling.

12

Mark Ward: Scoring Goals – Scoring Coke

What happens when a footballer's career ends? Most are forced to retire in their 30s, even though advances in fitness have extended the playing time of a lucky few. Of course, high-flyers like Beckham, Rooney and Ferdinand will probably never have any money worries at all. Others drift into TV, radio and press punditry. Many are swallowed up in the modern game's myriad of management and support services, from coaching to stress counselling to corporate hospitality and player representation. The sensible ones invest in more diverse businesses outside football to have something to fall back on just in case, everything from sportswear manufacturers and building companies to car dealerships, to name but a few. But for the majority of journeymen, unglamorous and largely unknown even to the vast majority of football fans, even in the Premiership, the future can be very chilly indeed. For the players whose names are rarely chanted by the crowd, retirement can mean financial hardship, lifestyle downsizing on a grand, often traumatic, scale and the cruel realisation that clubs don't give a loser's medal about them once they're past their sell-by dates, no matter how loyal and devoted they've been over the years. Business is business, at the end of the day, and football these days is definitely a business.

However, they may find one particular career path open to them – a job that doesn't require any qualifications, that has short but sometimes unsociable hours, and that, when it goes off, pays as well as can be. That career is gangsterism.

Former West Ham, Man City and Everton defender Mark Ward didn't exactly fill in a form at the jobcentre to secure his post as a drug-supplier. But he got the job anyway. And, until the day he got caught, he never looked back. The easy money was a lifeline during the dark days between formally hanging up his boots and desperately trying to find another way to make a living. Unfortunately, as he found out sooner rather than later, the holiday entitlement as a cocaine-dealer was longer than he had expected. Eight years, to be precise. At Her Majesty's pleasure.

Ward was jailed in 2005 after 4 kg (9 lb) of cocaine with a street value of up to £645,000 was discovered in a safe house he leased specifically to be used as a drugs factory and stash premises. After pleading guilty to possession with intent to supply, the 42 year old was sent to Walton Prison to serve out his sentence with plenty of boring days to ponder the time-honoured, riches-to-rags reverse football fable: where did it all go wrong?

Much of the information in this chapter is gleaned from court reports of Ward's case. However, many of the quotes from Ward himself and from some of his friends are taken from an exclusive interview he gave to Nick Harris of *The Independent*, first published in November 2005. Prisoner number NM6982 was born in Huyton, a tough area of Liverpool that had given rise to a galaxy of footballing heroes over the years, including, of course, Steven Gerrard. Ward was one of seven children from a working-class family. His labourer father got divorced from his mother, Irene, when Ward was 16, just as he was taking his tentative steps into major-league football. He joined Everton as a trainee but, in 1981, aged 18, he was dropped for being too small, too slow and less strong than his contemporaries. 'I was devastated. I knew I had the ability to make it. It was the worst moment of my career,' Ward said later.

He then joined non-league Northwich Victoria. In 1983, he played his first game at Wembley, in the FA Trophy final against Telford, but his team lost 2–1. Joe Royle, then the manager of Oldham, had seen Ward play and was impressed enough to sign him up for two years at £130 a week. Ward topped up his wages by working in a local bakery for an extra £70.

In 1985, West Ham's John Lyall paid £250,000 for Ward. The following season was one of the club's most successful – they finished third in Division One, their highest-ever position. Ironically, one of Ward's teammates was Frank McAvennie, later to be acquitted on a major drugs charge of his own. For Ward, these were the good times. By the time he was 23, he had a beautiful wife, Jane, a baby daughter, Melissa, a few quid in the bank and a big house down south.

Three years later, he moved to Howard Kendall's Manchester City for £1 million. Again, Ward helped to push his team to greater heights. In the 1990–91 season, fellow Scouser Peter Reid took the Sky Blues to fifth place – their highest position since 1978 and still unmatched. By this time, Kendall had moved to Ward's spiritual home, Everton, and in August 1991 he came looking for the Goodison reject made good. Ward was signed for £1.1 million and the most lucrative wages of his career, amounting to £2,000 a week.

'My home debut for Everton was the best moment of my career,' Ward told *The Independent* in his first press interview from behind bars. 'It had taken me ten years to get back to Everton, but I'd made it.' On the pitch, Ward rose to the occasion, and on the terraces the home-grown talent was a favourite with the fans, especially with the Blues' rowdier element. But the inner contentment of being back at home after all those years came with a price. Ward began celebrating his success in the local nightclubs, over the moon to go out with his mates and be amongst his own. However, he came into contact with gangsters.

During one ordeal, Ward was terrorised by flamboyant safe-cracker and contract-killer Charlie Seiga after a fracas in Liverpool's glitzy dance-round-your-handbag hotspot The Continental. Seiga claimed Ward, accompanied by a group of drunken Everton players, had severely disrupted an important business meeting he was holding with their rowdy and disrespectful behaviour. There was a bit of a go-around on the dance floor before the fight was broken up.

But that wasn't the end of it. The meeting was crucial, according to Seiga, as the business being discussed was a stepping stone on Seiga's road to long-awaited legitimacy. During the confrontation, Ward had stood up for himself, and bar-room threats were exchanged. They were not empty gestures. It was well known that Ward could handle himself. On the pitch, he was a no-nonsense hard-man. Plus, he had backup, whether he wanted it or not, amongst the fanatically Evertonian gangsters who were prepared to stand by him during a gangwar if it came to it. In addition, some of Ward's entourage had a bit of a reputation, and, what's more, they were juiced into Liverpool's newly emerging crime cartels then growing strong at an exponential rate on the back of the drugs trade.

At street level, Ward was also well connected. The Lacoste-clad scallywag-come-good had been adopted, mascot-style, by Everton's berserk hooligan following, known as The County Road Cutters and Kelly's Heroes, later to become the feared cocaine-fuelled Snorty Forty. Everton's top boys would faithfully follow Ward around Europe, whether he liked it or not, leaving a trail of robbery and violence behind them. Some of them claim that it was not uncommon for cash-rich Ward to buy their stolen swag, often exotic designer sportswear pilfered from some of Europe's most exclusive boutiques during games on the Continent. Ward would join this motley crew of drug-dealers, gangsters, doormen and scallies for late-night japery, especially on pre-season tours in far-flung parts of Europe.

But Seiga was not a man to be intimidated. Despite Ward's bad-lad credentials, nothing would save him from the sinister situation he now found himself in. Seiga put a contract on Ward's head and vowed to incapacitate the three Everton players who, he claimed, had publicly humiliated him. They were going to be put under manners big-time.

Hothead Seiga began turning up at Everton's training ground with a kitchen knife secreted under his £750 suit jacket. He maintained his one-man siege for a week. The strength and morale of the Everton squad went into free-fall, according to insiders. On the first day, the four players, including Ward, who had been warned that Seiga lay in wait didn't turn up.

More players began giving training a wide berth after they were threatened by Seiga, demanding to know where Ward and his mates were hiding. Eventually, the situation reached crisis point. Everton manger Howard Kendall was forced to call one of his contacts in a bid to negotiate an end to hostilities. The middlemen called Seiga and begged him to back off as it was ruining the Blues' chances of league and cup victory.

Seiga agreed to stop staking out the training ground but remained insistent that Ward would be dead on sight. He wasn't, Seiga warned, getting a 'walkover'. Revenge was imminent. The middlemen advised Ward that he was still in danger.

Meanwhile, a Merseyside godfather, who was also a fanatical Evertonian, got wind of Ward's predicament. At the time, this gangster, whom we shall call The Restaurateur because he owned a high-class eaterie among his wide business interests, was a senior but autonomous distributor in Curtis Warren's hugely successful cocaine cartel. Today, with Warren inside, he has taken over as one of Britain's biggest drug-dealers, worth tens of millions of pounds. The Restaurateur agreed to a sit-down with Seiga to smooth things over, which he did. Seiga was allowed to save face. Ward was allowed to save his life.

In return for this service to Ward, The Restaurateur was awarded favours. Though Ward did not know he was a gangster, he thanked the businessman for his help. Years later, after Ward had finished his playing career for Everton and Altrincham, he was persuaded by his rescuer to play in a non-league Sunday team that he sponsored. Ward obliged.

After Everton, Ward's Premiership career lasted another two and a half years. At 31, he moved to Birmingham as a player–coach. Despite sudden relegation, the Ward effect helped them bounce back the following season, together with an Auto Windscreens Trophy triumph at Wembley. As a professional whose pursuit of success had bridged the eras either side of the Premiership's birth, he was not ready to retire from football yet, and when he did he assumed there would be a prosperous post-playing career of some description.

But career-wise the end was nigh. He was getting on a bit and his glory days were behind him. The big wages (nowhere near as big as today, but relatively good) were all over. The stress began to pile up. After 14 years, he and Jane got divorced. With gritted teeth, Ward battled on, playing here and there, wherever he could. He landed contracts with Huddersfield and Wigan. But one day he badly injured his hand. Still he would not give it up. Wigan wouldn't allow him to play until the injury healed and the metal wiring in his hand was taken out. But Dundee, unaware of the injury, wanted a midfielder for one game. Foolishly, he cut off the exposed wires himself, covered his hand and drove to Scotland in a last-ditch attempt to hang on to all he knew. But hours after the game, infection struck. He was hospitalised for six days. That was the full stop at the end of his official playing career.

By the end of 1996, after 11 years of playing, he was facing financial ruin. His wife had got the house in the divorce settlement and his pension was virtually worthless. The investments he had put away for a rainy day, mainly property, had been wiped out by negative equity during the '90s house-price crash. He told *The Independent*, 'I had a pension, but to be honest I didn't put as much into it as I perhaps should have. Don't get me wrong; I had a good life, a comfortable life, while I was playing. The house, the car, the social life. I didn't worry too much about spending what I earned. But I didn't really think there'd be a time when I'd have no job at all. I suppose I thought I'd always be able to make a living from football. But when you don't get that job you want, it's not like that. There was no significant income to speak of. I don't want anyone's sympathy; it's just the reality.'

Optimistically, Ward had half his working life ahead of him to retrain and start a new career. But he could not break his addiction to football.

In 1997, Ward went to Australia to start up a footballing academy and possibly break into a team there. But he soon returned and tried some radio commentating. Outwardly, he maintained a front to the world that he was still riding high, playing in Masters events, doing charity shows and opening the odd local event. Then came his last chance to stay in the football industry: a player–manager's job at Altrincham. But just over a year later, his world came crashing down beyond repair when he was sacked over disagreements with the chairman. The ordeal was a blow to his whole existence. Weeks later, instead of signing autographs, he was signing on the dole.

Still the stubborn player, who had always been described as one of life's triers, refused to give up the footballing dream. In 2004, he scrabbled some airfare and spends together for a last-ditch trip to Oz. But when his ventures collapsed and his visa ran out, he was forced to return to Liverpool.

In November 2004, Ward was rushed to hospital with suspected viral meningitis and various acute stress disorders. His life was upside down. He was crashing in his girlfriend's pad one night, his mother's or his mate's the next. Crimbo was looming; there was no dough in his backbin. Warm memories of cheery and cash-rich Christmases past, when life was good and his ex-wife had her own horse, were haunting his grim and troubled psyche.

Out of the blue, a fairy godfather came to his rescue. An associate lent him £500. Later, the kindly benefactor came with a proposition that would help pay off the debt and get him more wages to boot. He wanted Ward to rent a semi-detached house in Prescot, on behalf of someone else. At first, Ward refused, sensing something half-shady. But after Christmas left him skint, and the depressive clouds of January set in, he changed his tune. 'My financial situation had become so dire that I agreed. I knew the house was going to be used for a "stash". It could've been anything: drugs, cigarettes, money, and, to be honest, I didn't care. All I had to do was rent it and provide access. I never even lived there.'

Ward's job was to keep the place safe and normal to the outside world: tidy up, make it seem lived in, report any suspicious activity. He had become, knowingly or unknowingly, a cog in a multibillion-pound drugs business, one of the thousands of support workers who help to get narcotics from A to B and on the market in a safe and saleable manner in today's highly efficient trade. Ward told Nick Harris, 'I went round one day to check on the place and couldn't believe the mess it was in. There was powder, bowls, plastic bags, all kinds of drugs paraphernalia. I just thought, "What the hell have I got involved in?"

'I spoke to the guy and said, "That's it; I want out." I knew I was in big trouble if it all came out. I tried in vain to escape from the situation but was told to shut up and let the tenancy agreement run its course until July. I knew I'd just have to sit tight. I was paid between £400 and £500 a week to rent the property. I was still hoping to return to Australia. I was at the lowest I've ever been in my life. I got into something that I should never have gone near. I made a terrible, terrible mistake. And there just wasn't any way to get out of it.'

Four months later, at 11.15 a.m. on 12 May 2005, police raided the house. More than 3 kg of pure cocaine, with an estimated street value of £645,000, were recovered, along with bowls, mixing agents, a vacuum seal and a hydraulic press – the easily transportable materials and machinery that make up a modern drugs factory. Cocaine was caked on almost every available surface – on the bowls and dishes in the kitchen, on the knives and the wooden spoons in the sink, on the draining board and the electric food mixer – and it even dusted the table like poisoned icing sugar. The police did not know about Ward's involvement at first, but the paper trail inside the house led to him within minutes.

On the morning in question, Ward had received a phone call from the estate agent telling him the alarm had gone off and the police were outside. He sneaked past the address, realised it wasn't a routine check and tried to get off immediately, bottle gone. His MGF sports car slowed, pausing for a moment, only to accelerate away again. Unfortunately, he had stopped long enough for officers to recognise his face. And they could not believe their luck. He had already been named on a note found inside, and one enterprising officer called the firm letting the property and asked them to inform the tenant his alarm was ringing out – that had been a deliberate ploy.

And so, the police watched as Ward was duped into driving back to his cocaine den in the middle of a drugs bust. In a panic, the footballer abandoned his car and attempted to mingle with construction workers while pretending to talk on his mobile telephone, but the next call Ward would be making was to his lawyer. The police had followed from the house and arrested him without ceremony. He didn't attempt to run or deny it, as if in a bid to salvage some honour and truth from the very bad situation. As always, he was prepared to take responsibility. Ward admitted knowing that the drugs were on the premises but denied that he was the owner of the stash.

Initially, he faced three charges, including possession of crack cocaine and intent to supply it. Those two were dropped because the forensic evidence did not stack up. In court, Ward was described as a 'foot soldier'. The prosecution argued that he was a dealer, based on evidence of traces of cocaine in the boot of his car, his washbag being in the house and one telephone message from someone saying they were 'pissed' and needed 'a line'.

Ward's barrister, Nicholas Johnson, summed up the inglorious end to his playing career when he explained how he had become 'a convicted drug-trafficker'.

Mr Johnson added: 'When he played professional football, he earned a good living, but by present-day standards the money did not bear comparison. At the height of his career with Everton, he was earning £1,200 a week. When it came to retirement, he had no healthy bank balance, no business interests and no rosy career as a media pundit.' A forensic inspection uncovered traces of cocaine all over the boot of Ward's car. Not only had he known his premises were being used to traffic drugs, not only was he being solicited for cocaine, but it was apparent the car had been used to deliver it, too.

'Ward tried to stick to his story that he was not part of this drugs ring, but that soon changed when the evidence made it clear there was a lot more to it,' said DI Chris Green, of Merseyside Police.

Judge John Phipps said, 'It is regrettable to see a former professional footballer of your ability reduced to this.'

Ward did not fold under questioning. He refused to grass up his bosses 'because of the chance of repercussions'.

A close friend added: 'He could have cut a deal for a lighter sentence by throwing in the rest of the gang to the police. But that would have meant death, or life on the witness-protection programme. You choose. So he stayed staunch and got his head down.'

Ward reflected in his interview with Nick Harris: 'I feel gutted at what I've done. I feel ashamed that I got involved and embarrassed at the stigma of receiving an eight-year sentence. I did something that was against all my principles. It's a part of my life that's unimaginable. I will always regret it. Being taken away from your loved ones is the worst feeling. My daughter's twenty-two now, and I've got three grandchildren – one born since I've been inside. What have I done to my daughter with all this? Your dad's supposed to be your hero. I've shattered that.

'If anything good can come from this, from this situation I've brought upon myself, then I hope others will realise the consequences of getting involved in something like this. I've messed up my life.'

On a visit to a hospital outside prison, Ward understood the significance of his situation as Everton fans gawped at him handcuffed to two prison officers. 'What must anyone who saw me think I've done?' he says. 'I was beyond embarrassed. I could've been a terrorist. I could've been a serial killer. That's what I've come to.

'It will take a brave man to employ me in any capacity after this horrendous experience. But I'm staying positive, and hope by the time I'm released, I can look forward to the rest of my days.'

At the beginning of 2006, he was transferred from Walton Prison in Liverpool to Buckley Hall, Lancashire, and could be released on a tag at the end of 2008. However, he may be given extra time if a judge decides that 'proceeds of crime' are owed to the state and cannot be paid for. Ward's legal representative, Len Font, from the Liverpool law firm Hogan Brown Solicitors, says that Ward 'has nothing'.

Ward's case is fascinating because it shows how quickly a player can descend to the depths when he is influenced by criminals. All players find it difficult to adjust, but perhaps if the underworld influence in football wasn't quite as strong as it is then Ward may have been able to find a legit way of making a living. The other interesting aspect was how his former colleagues and bosses reacted. More often than not, they were sympathetic and, as always with footy folk, philosophical. Some, who had obviously come across the underworld influence in football, were realistic about its hugely negative effect on players. Some pointed out that Ward had never shown any signs of being mixed up with crime.

Former West Ham boss Lou Macari reacted with disbelief. He said, 'It's a massive surprise. Mark was a handy player and he never caused me any problems, other than the usual arguments that you get with any player from time to time. Off the pitch, there were certainly no instances of me having to speak to him about things away from the club, and there were never any problems with people that he associated with.

'He was a popular player with the supporters and with the players. It's really sad that Mark has ended up in this situation, and I'm disappointed in him.'

Andy Hinchcliffe, a former England left-back whose playing career ended prematurely because of injury, had greater sympathy for him, born out of personal experience. Though Hinchcliffe did not resort to criminality, he had found it difficult to adjust. He said, 'I experienced a difficult six months myself when I finished playing. When you stop, it takes you time to become accustomed to your new life, and it takes you time to move on mentally. Players are still very young when they finish playing, and it can be hard to fill your time.

'There is a lot of pressure on you to do something else, but that can be difficult for players who have only ever played football, and some people obviously get involved in the wrong kind of thing.

'When you drop out of the game, you realise you are not a superstar and you never were. I found it very hard in the first few months. Many can't adapt.

'How do you cope with starting again? Do you sit behind a desk? Do you go back to college? For a lot, it's an ego thing. I can sympathise with people like Mark who fall in with the wrong crowd. He won't be the last to do it.'

Gordon Taylor, the chief executive of the Professional Footballers' Association, hoped that learning was the key to keeping players on the right road: 'We have extensive education programmes about planning for the future and warning of the dangers of getting involved with drugs, in any capacity. Mark Ward's case should be a warning to all players, of all ages, to be prepared for that cold day of reckoning when your playing career is over.'

'You couldn't ask for a better professional,' said former manager Howard Kendall. 'He was fiery, but there was no hint of anything else.'

Tony Cottee, a former teammate at West Ham and Everton and now a Sky Sports analyst, said, 'The Boys of '86 [West Ham's glory players from that season's side] has been very important to us. We created a company to stage golf days, other events, to raise a bit of money for some of the lads who'd fallen on hard times. We're talking about a few hundred pounds here and there.

'I was aware Wardy was struggling, of the financial problems. I was as unaware as anyone else about the trouble he was getting into.

'What I've said to him in letters is he needs to get his head down, do a computer course or something if he can, write his memoirs, sort his education. Most footballers, me included, don't pay attention to it during their playing days. It's important Wardy learns from his mistake.

'You can see how financial problems arise. Players from a whole era of the game, the '60s, '70s, '80s, even the early '90s, we didn't retire with so much money we didn't need to work again. If Wardy was playing now, he'd be earning £25,000 or £30,000 a week.'

Former manager Joe Royle added: 'He was the best non-League player I'd seen. He impressed me so much with his enthusiasm, his energy, his confidence. From the first moment, he was terrific, so good, not an ounce of trouble, a bright personality. He was a great kid. I'm sure at his peak he must've been considered for an England cap.

'I feel for him. It goes without saying, we all abhor the drugs trade. But in my experience of Mark, he must've been pretty desperate. I was astounded. It's sad. He's lost everything as quick as he gained it. It's a terrible shame. I only hope things work out for him.'

Former Birmingham boss Barry Fry said, 'I had a row with Mark because he liked a drink, and he liked a bet and I fined him for something that will stay between me and him. [Ward says this was probably an occasion when he went out drinking and got involved in a nightclub fracas.] But a footballer having a drink and a bet is not new, is it? No player likes it when you fine him.

'But when people ask me who was the best player I had at Birmingham, was it Liam Daish, who I bought for £50,000 and sold for £150,000, or Jose Dominguez, who I bought for £180,000 and sold for £1.4 million, or this player or that player who I made big money on? No, I'll tell you. The best player I ever had was Mark Ward.

'As a player, as an influence on the team on the pitch, he was different class. Did I think he had the potential to be a manager? Yes. He had an opinion. He was strong, mentally and physically. I think I even recommended him later when he was looking for a management job in the non-League.

'I'm not surprised that he's taken the stance to own up to whatever he's done wrong. To be fair to him, that was his attitude as a player. If he fucked up, he put his hands up and admitted it.'

13

Retraining for Rackets: Mickey Thomas and Stephen Cole

One of the most difficult periods for footballers in recent years was the late '80s and early '90s, around the same time as the old leagues switched to the Premier League and so on. The birth of the Premiership marked a financial windfall of oil-wildcatting proportions for the top clubs. By the end of the millennium, successful players had gone from earning £60,000 a year to £60,000 a week in some cases.

But many players simply missed the boat. They formed part of the unlucky few whose careers reached a peak in the late '80s and early '90s, and by the time the boom came about they were ready to retire. They missed out on the super-money by a whisker. And for them they could only stand on the sidelines and watch in bemused wonder.

At the same time, there was a similar change going on in organised crime in Britain. Drugs had arrived en masse on these shores and changed the criminal landscape beyond recognition. Suddenly, organised crime began to generate billions of pounds, as opposed to millions, and relatively low-ranking villains became super-wealthy almost overnight. Many of the armed robbers who had sat at the top of the criminal hierarchy in the '70s and early '80s switched to drugs and became very rich.

FOOTBALL AND GANGSTERS

A number of economic factors had helped to stimulate a massive boom in the drugs trade, such as the industrial harvesting of narco crops, which made them cheap to make. The boom in investment property made it easier for drug-barons to wash money. Banking deregulation and the big bang made drug transactions user-friendly and hiding the profits more simple. Dealers using new electronic services could transfer large amounts of money quicker, cheaper and more anonymously than ever before, avoiding paper trails and disguising origins by bouncing balances through multiple accounts all over the world. Offshore accounts became more accessible. New laws and computerised trading allowed small companies to trade shares without having to go through traditional stockbrokers. The freer markets also offered a vast range of investments in which to secrete and benefit from bent cash. High-risk futures trading, junk bonds and emerging specialist markets, such as technology stocks, were perfect vehicles for organised criminals to turn dirty money into legit profits and losses. Booming fund markets made it easier for villains to slip a few million into multibillion-pound portfolios. As foreign markets opened up, drugs earnings from Britain's streets began propping up a range of shady businesses, from Caspian oil companies to Middle Eastern banks. Technological advancements in mobile phones, pagers and cheap air travel also helped dealers logistically. And the recession of the early '80s in many British cities made sure that there was a willing army of foot soldiers available to work for the cartels – as well as a ready-made pool of disaffected young people to consume the drugs they were selling.

The following examples reflect these changes and go some way to illustrating how some players moved into more and more serious crimes as the underworld itself became more sinister and deadly. Early on, players like Mickey Thomas turned to traditional crimes such as counterfeiting money. But, as the stakes became higher in the criminal world and drugs took over, some of the new wave of unemployed soccer stars such as Stephen Foley were being accused of getting mixed up in the deadly trade as well. The end result was that former players, such as Stephen Cole, were taking bigger and bigger risks – a decision which eventually cost him his life in a horrific machete attack.

Michael Reginald Thomas debuted for Wrexham in the '70s. His talent soon took him to Man United for more than £300,000 in 1978, where he played for three years. Mickey became known as the Welsh George Best for his off-the-field antics, which included the usual – Page 3 girls and booze – and the not so usual, such as being stabbed in the bum by his former brother-in-law as he shagged the brother-in-law's new missus in a car up a country lane.

After bouts at Everton, Chelsea and Leeds, he returned to Wrexham to plan his retirement from the game practically skint in 1992. But not before he helped the Fourth Division lager-sponsored Reds knock Arsenal, the League champions, out of the FA Cup in 1992 with a godlike, unforgettable free-kick. Thomas could do no wrong. Except commit crime. He invested his time and energy in a printing press to make counterfeit money. He started passing fake £10 notes to trainees at the club to get rid of, and it wasn't long before he was caught. In 1993, he got 18 months in jail. Judge Gareth Edwards had condemned the player's misguided image of himself as a 'flash and daring adventurer'. Thomas thought he was getting a walkout. He joked with the court reporters, 'Anyone got change of a tenner for the phone?' But it ended up with him being taken away in a prison van. 'The judge made an example of me,' he said. 'He was enjoying it: a full house, with all the media there. If I'd been anyone else, I probably wouldn't have gone to jail.'

In Walton Prison, his cellmate had killed two people – then cut off their heads. 'Walton Prison, in Liverpool, was tough, but after that I had it quite comfortable inside,' said the ex-Welsh international. The long-haired midfielder was used to the good life. He made sure he had the best of everything: drink, plenty of days at home, nice car. Thomas's life behind bars was so cushy that the *News of the World* got wind of it and turned him over. The Screws (the Fleet Street nickname for the Sunday newspaper, not the prison officers) splashed on a photo of him swigging from a champagne bottle and a story warning that the picture 'will enrage every law-abiding Briton'.

Today, Thomas is a successful radio pundit and after-dinner speaker. In one of his best lines, the irony of the changing world of football is not lost on him. 'Roy Keane's on fifty grand a week. Mind you, so was I until the police found my printing machine.'

Thomas was lucky in a way. Though he had just missed out on the silly-money wages of footy, he got nicked just before the mid-'90s drugs boom took off. His criminality was nipped in the bud before the temptation to dabble in drugs had even arisen.

Only a few years later, former Liverpool footballer Stephen Foley was to be accused of being in a drugs gang. When he was arrested with £57,890 in a plastic bag, he had some explaining to do. Police surveillance teams had suspected Foley was a key player in the busy Glasgow and Liverpool drugs network. Foley had been an Anfield starlet during the club's 1980s heyday – when the line-up included legends Kenny Dalglish, Ian Rush and Alan Hansen. But he didn't quite survive the upheaval of the Premiership, and by March 2000, when he booked into Glasgow's Hilton Hotel with his partner Lynden Nowell – under the name Jones – his footballing days were over.

Cops watched the pair all day and claimed they saw them mixing with known drug-dealers. That evening, detectives pounced at the city's Queen Street railway station. The bag full of cash was seized. Three months later, police swooped on the Maryhill flat of Stephen Dickson. Inside were Dickson, Colin Wilson and Foley, who was in the bedroom with heroin worth £500,000 and plastic bags over his hands. Foley gave his brother's name to police to avoid being identified, and the officers found a further £930 in his hired car. Wilson and Dickson were both jailed. Foley, then 42, said he had won the money at Ascot and produced betting slips to support the story. But on the days Foley said he was winning, he was found to be elsewhere.

The drugs case was temporarily dropped while the Crown decided whether to prosecute him for attempting to pervert the course of justice. Foley, who also played for Stoke City, finally stood trial on the drugs charges in November 2005. Ex-Celtic ace and former Stoke manager Lou Macari was listed as a defence witness but did not give evidence. Unemployed Foley got one of the biggest results of his career when he walked free after a verdict of not proven. Investigators found that Foley receives a Professional Footballers' Association pension of £236 a month, £9,600 a year income support and incapacity benefit of £1,201 a year.

By the mid- to late-'90s, a growing number of cash-strapped former professional footballers from all corners of the country were heavily involved in the drugs business. Many of them chose to be at the dangerous cutting edge, taking increasingly bigger risks in a bid to plug the holes in their poorly managed finances. The motivation was a dangerous mix of competitive sporting psychology and personal emotions born of their recent life changes. An underworld source described how one fairly well-known player got involved in growing skunk cannabis – in his own property. The source said, 'This guy owned a building which he and his partners converted into a huge loft growing cannabis. The fella was taking a big risk, because he was famous, at the end the day. Everyone knew this place was his and the police were finding these things all the time. The technology wasn't around then like it is today to disguise things like the loads of electricity that's needed or the purifiers which take the smells away. But the money was very good. He was making about £5,000 to £10,000 a week off that and other things which come your way when you go down that route.

'It was ontop to death, but he was greedy. It was only a matter of time before it got raided, but he kept pushing it. He wanted to be the main boy. He actually thought he could take the proper gangsters on. Madness. The main thing behind that was that he was really bitter that he'd left his job with no money. He couldn't handle being a loser. That was it. I remember him saying that if he was playing nowadays, he'd be a millionaire. It was though he was trying to make up for lost time. In the end, his partner got caught and got 14 years. It was this player's fault, but his mate paid the price. The player had a lucky escape, because he said he didn't know it was going on and the busies believed him.'

Another ex-footballer – a former Division One senior player and successful international who also went on to be a club exec – invested his cash in heroin for a period in the late '90s when it looked like he wouldn't get another job and his marriage had failed. The player teamed up with a bent lawyer and several very nasty gangsters, and it's not known whether he knew how they were investing his money, but it was used to fund class-A drug deals.

Many players also got involved in the numerous support industries connected to the drugs trade. In the late '90s, security companies became the building blocks of organised crime in Britain. Suddenly, companies that provided bouncers to nightclubs became rich, powerful and violent because they realised that if they controlled the doors on clubs, they controlled the drugs supply.

Former Liverpool pro Stephen Cole became a bouncer. Though he didn't deal drugs, he got mixed up in the internecine squabbles between the rival door firms. When a dispute spiralled out of control, two opposing door teams 'called out' their finest troops and deployed them in a series of strike raids on enemy pubs and clubs. One well-known senior bouncer was stabbed in an attack on a premises he was contracted to defend. Cole's name was 'thrown into the hat' as one of the instigators, and in revenge he was macheted to death by two squads of eight to ten doormen, who attacked him almost simultaneously in a coordinated manoeuvre. He was targeted because he was vulnerable. The gang were tipped off that Cole was out drinking with his wife without the protection of his doormen associates. The mystery assailants used baseball bats, swords, knives and cleavers to batter him and hack off his head, arms and legs while he enjoyed a Sunday-evening pint with his wife. She looked on as the gang chopped and stabbed her husband to shreds in an orgy of blood-curdling violence, astonishingly carried out in front of a packed pub. The drinkers were subdued with CS gas as the men went to work. The attack was all the more shocking because the pub was not known for its gangland connections, and the customers who witnessed it were regarded as 'civilians'.

Lorraine Cole, the deceased's wife, told a court later that she saw a man called John Riley attacking her husband after she had been sprayed directly in the face with CS gas. Cole's death was attributed to a blow to the head with a baseball bat and multiple stab wounds. Riley was sentenced to life with a minimum of 20 years, but his family claim it was mistaken identity. A second assailant, Robert McCarthy, 48, was also jailed for life at Preston Crown Court in 1997 after being found guilty of killing Cole, and several other villains were convicted of various other offences connected to the attack.

14

Scottish Soccer: a Gangsters' Paradise

In recent years, the Scottish leagues have been plagued by an influx of gangsterism on a worrying scale. The exact reasons for the unusually large impact are unclear, but sources within the game say that the close-knit, highly concentrated nature of both football and the underworld in Scotland have allowed influences to cross-fertilise rapidly, unlike in England, where the expansion of gangsters into the clubs has been more subtle and longer-term. A long-standing, senior executive in Scottish football said, 'Football and the underworld have always lived side by side in Scotland in a pressure-cooker atmosphere – especially in Glasgow, where a lot of the well-known characters have followed the teams for years.'

Other professionals of the sport believe that the Old Firm rivalries and the links of extreme factions of supporters to paramilitaries in Northern Ireland have exacerbated the problem. A former footballer said, 'It's no big secret that gangsters have been attracted to some of the smaller clubs in Scotland to launder money, just like anywhere. In other places, they've grown close to the bigger clubs because of the prestige it brings them – after all, in some Scottish cities there's no bigger status symbols than the clubs, and gangsters love being associated with the power and the razzmatazz. But you've also got to take account of things like the hooligans, which have given rise to gangsters such as Billy McPhee, or the links to the UDA and the IRA by certain elements in Glasgow. A lot of business is done at the match. Gun-running and drug-dealing in Scotland owes a lot to the bonds made through football. It's networking.'

There is a lot of evidence to show how the Scottish game has become infected by organised crime. Frankie 'Donuts' Donaldson has made millions from smuggling drugs and booze. But despite a criminal record stretching back 20 years, he became a non-executive director for Raith Rovers and was at the centre of a long-running Inland Revenue probe surrounding the investment. Shocked Raith Rovers bosses had no idea that Donuts was a wrong 'un and that the lifelong Celtic fan's influence was felt far beyond the boardroom. The crimelord is worth an estimated £3.3 million, and when he heard that a former top Scottish player had allegedly indecently assaulted his daughter, he blew his top. And put a contract out on the star. The player was taxed, even though the allegations were never proved and no charges were ever brought against the player. The crimelord's daughter was also allowed an all-expenses-paid spending spree at Glasgow's Armani shop.

Former terrace casual Billy McPhee never lost his passion for football – even though he became one of Glasgow's most feared east-end enforcers. McPhee graduated from hooliganism, along with hard-man Gordon Ross, to become an underboss for Thomas 'The Licensee' McGraw. But McPhee's life was inextricably linked with football. Dozens of Scottish players past and present were his friends.

McPhee's fellow McGraw henchman Gordon Ross was stabbed to death outside a pub in Shettleston. Then an attempt was made on McPhee's life as he drank in the Shettleston Juniors Social Club. The father of two from Barlanark was finally hacked to death in a crowded restaurant, six weeks after Ross's slaying. McPhee had been watching the Scotland v. Wales rugby game just before he was killed. But his pals say he was talking about his beloved football right up to the last minute of his life. Later, the man accused of murdering him walked free from court after the charge against him was withdrawn. Mark Clinton had been accused of repeatedly and fatally stabbing McPhee in front of horrified diners at the Brewers Fayre in Baillieston. The case collapsed after crucial identification evidence from two eyewitnesses was deemed insufficient.

It was a cruel irony. Police had been after McPhee for the gangland attack on fellow Glasgow crime figure T.C. Campbell. T.C. had recently been released from prison on appeal after being cleared of murder during the city's infamous Ice-Cream Wars. Officers, like all of the Scottish underworld, knew it was McPhee, but the investigation repeatedly fell apart when witnesses were too petrified to ID him. McPhee was part of a small and vicious world in Glasgow's drug trade, with all of the players known to each other – often having been best pals – as well as to the police. McPhee had attacked T.C., police believe, simply as an action to reinstate McGraw's failing power on the streets, rather than as an assassination attempt. 'McGraw looked about for some muppet he could hit,' said a senior officer in the investigation. 'It's a bit like being a vandal and putting something up on the wall – making a statement about yourself and what you can do.'

Sensible footballers plan ahead for their futures beyond football. Canny Scottish ones are often amongst the most successful at making businesses pay off – take former Rangers player Gordon Ramsay, who went from a downer injury to a super-successful career as a restaurateur, celebrity chef and problem-solver. He took the best parts of football and Scotland – competitiveness, straight-talking, hard work and an eye on the bottom line – and struck gold when other has-been, write-off players would have turned to drink and drugs. If the Scots can't do business, no one can. There are more millionaires per head in Edinburgh than in any other part of Europe. It's no coincidence that the most successful chancellor in British history is a Scotchlander!

But when footballers go into business with Scotland's other greatest export – villains – then it all seems to go skew-whiff. Always. When former Celtic and Arsenal hero Charlie Nicholas sunk his life savings into a pub run by family friend and well-known 'community leader' Jim Milligan, he hoped that the investment would bloom into a chain of 20 or 50, which they could sell for a premium after his playing days were over. Of course, Nicholas did not know of his partner's criminal background.

Initially, they got off to a good start. Their business ran various pubs, including the Café Cini chain, the New Morven and Thompson's bar in Glasgow's Springburn area. They were rising stars on the pub scene. Their Café Cini bar in Glasgow sponsored snooker player Mark Williams and it was a haunt for footballers from Celtic and Rangers. The next move included a £5 million 'Planet Football' restaurant. But their ambitious plans were soon to lie in ruins. Things started to go downhill when increasing underworld influences began to eclipse Nicholas's good business image. Milligan had attracted investment capital from a gangster family called the McGoverns. But when a feud broke out between the McGoverns and a gangland rival, Nicholas and Milligan got caught up in the crossfire and their Café Cini bar in Greenock was set on fire.

Predictably, all of the money soon went down the drain. The business crashed, Nicholas was left holding £300,000 worth of debt and, to boot, the McGovern crew, known as the Springburn Sopranos on the street, appeared on the scene claiming that Jim owed them a further £1 million. Equally predictably, old Jim disappeared over the horizon, feigning ignorance. Sightings were reported in New Zealand, Australia and America.

Charlie was facing one of the toughest tests of his life. He had a lot of explaining to do. First off, he blamed the mess on old Jim. He said that the signatures on the loan agreements laid on by the brewery were not his. Guess whose they were? Yes, you've guessed it. Charlie said he had been back-doored by Jim, that he had not been told about the hundreds of thousands of pounds in crisis-cash handed over by the brewery and that Jim had unlawfully put his name to the documents.

By now, Charlie was a telly pundit for Sky Sports, earning around £300,000 a year for his work. In February 2005, Nicholas went to court to try to avoid having to pay the £318,300 to Interbrew. In the Court of Session in Edinburgh, he asked to have the loan guarantees invalidated due to the allegedly forged signatures. The 43 year old told the court he hadn't signed the documents. He said his signature had been forged by Milligan in 1999 and 2000. The former Scotland international also said in his action that he would be liable to sequestration if the payment was not suspended.

Nicholas told the court that Milligan had disappeared, and, when asked if he knew where his former business associate was, he said, 'I haven't a clue.' He explained how he had invested in a pub business with Milligan in the late 1980s when he was still playing football. The duo planned to buy 'a substantial number of pubs' and sell them, but their firm, Jimmy Nicks Properties Ltd, eventually went into receivership, costing the ex-striker approximately £70,000. He said he was earning about £75,000 a year as a footballer at the time, and it was his only investment, apart from paying into a pension. He said that Milligan, a close family friend, had been responsible for running the business and explained, 'It was only a verbal agreement that the two of us would go into business together and he would control it. Looking back now, it was a silly risk. I was probably young and naive at the time, but it was something I wanted to do.'

He said he'd learned that the firm had got into difficulties, but he had not been told he would be required to give a personal guarantee to the brewers over loans made. Nicholas added that he had previously raised legal proceedings relating to Milligan and personal guarantees in the 1990s, which had been settled. He explained, 'It was basically a case that he had signed my signature.' Asked if he was aware that Mr Milligan had needed to raise further funds from the brewers in 2000, he replied, 'No, I was not aware he was requiring funds. He said at the time he had a problem with VAT, but that's as much as I know.'

Nicholas later discovered that the Clydesdale Bank also had personal guarantees which were allegedly signed by him, but it had not taken any steps over them. Milligan, in order to help his old mate's case, even wrote a letter to Nicholas's lawyers confessing that he had faked the signatures. In it, he said, 'I hereby write to confirm to you that I, Jim Milligan, residing in Southern Ireland, signed Charlie Nicholas's PG letters of consent. He had no knowledge, as he'd told me in the past that he would never sign another PG agreement. I had no option, as we would not get the loan without his signature. I enclose his so-called signature, which is mine. So I think your handwriting specialists should try another job. Charlie, I am sorry for putting you through this. I did not intend for things to end up like they have.' Nicholas's lawyers lodged this sworn statement with the court. Lord Menzies was expected to give a written judgement at a later date.

But Jim had more worrying issues than a bank on his case. The gangsters who said that he owed them a million were trying to find him as well. The McGoverns had had a large financial interest in his firm, Jimmy Nicks, when it crashed and were left with nothing after Milligan fled. To make matters worse, the police were also hovering around after taking an interest in Nicholas's case. They wanted to quiz Milligan about the allegation of fraudulent signatures, if the court battle proved that indeed the signature was counterfeit. In addition, Milligan was being hunted by receivers Kroll Buchler Phillips over the collapse of the business venture. He quickly became Scotland's most wanted man. But the shameless rogue fronted it out. Cheekily, he kept slipping back into Glasgow, under the noses of gangsters out to kill him. On one visit, he revealed to the *Sunday Mail* newspaper that he had been hiding in Ireland. He brushed off the underworld threats, boasting that he had nothing to fear from the McGovern clan. He said, 'They are finished. I am under no fear from [them]. As far as I am concerned, they are finished.'

Ironically, the McGovern family had once been the source of his good fortune. Their wealth and power had allowed Milligan to grow. But his world fell apart when his associate Tony McGovern was shot dead outside one of his pubs, the New Morven in Barlanark, Glasgow. Milligan told the *Sunday Mail*: 'I have always wanted to speak about that side of my life, but that time is not now.' Milligan had disappeared in February 2001, just before his and Nicholas's firm went bust. Milligan added: 'I want to see how Charlie gets on with his case. I am planning to give my side of it because of the rubbish that has been written about me.

'I am only back to do a couple of bits of business. I am based in Ireland, not Australia and New Zealand, as has been said. I do not know where this has come from. Ireland is my place.'

During Nicholas's civil action, the court heard how Milligan had refused to attend, fearing arrest for fraud and because there were 'people who want to find him'. After McGovern was killed, Milligan was visited by thugs who wanted to replace his staff with their own people and take over the tills. Nicholas could easily have been a target. Accountant Richard Cleary, 33, who managed the books for Jimmy Nicks at the time it went bust, told the court: 'I feared for my own safety. It was scary stuff.'

Milligan's home in Gartcosh, Lanarkshire, was trashed by the McGoverns. The windows were smashed, the electric gates destroyed and the house covered in graffiti.

Although the police's prime suspect initially had been Jamie Stevenson, a former close friend, there was little evidence to support this and no charges were brought against him. Robin Macpherson, a lawyer who has worked for Nicholas, said he met Milligan at a hotel near Edinburgh Airport in September. He said Milligan confessed to twice faking Nicholas's signature. Macpherson added: 'He asked me what likely sentence he would receive if he ended up in court. Given we were talking of frauds of over £300,000, I thought it was pretty likely he would receive a custodial sentence.'

Milligan told him his troubles started 'after Tony [McGovern] was shot outside the bar'.

Macpherson added: 'As I understand it, while Tony McGovern was alive, these other people who caused trouble for Mr Milligan were kept under control by McGovern.'

In May 2005, a Scots football financier and former business partner of Terry Venables became the number-one target in a multimillion-pound money-laundering investigation. Lawrence Gillick, 60, son of the Rangers football legend Torry, was questioned by detectives from the Scottish Drugs Enforcement Agency (SDEA) following the seizure of £7 million from a Glasgow bank account – the largest made in Scotland under the Proceeds of Crime Act. Detectives believed the money had been sent to Scotland as part of a laundering scam involving transfers between accounts in Latvia, Hungary, Russia, America and Scotland in 2003. Former bankrupt Gillick, who teamed up with Venables in a failed bid to buy Tottenham Hotspur in 1991, attempted to transfer the funds into his company account. Police froze the assets following a tip-off from the Royal Bank of Scotland.

Gillick was quizzed but was not charged with an offence and denied any wrongdoing. He has been linked to a number of business failures and an investment scheme which led to huge losses for a major British charity. A greyhound-racing complex in Ayr which went wrong bankrupted him. A number of other sports-related ventures in London also went down the pan.

Gillick then teamed up with Venables in an attempt to buy Spurs. The Scots financier claimed that he could raise £10 million to buy the club but the bid fell through after it emerged that Gillick did not have the funds. The financier vanished and was reported to have been murdered by gangsters. Nevertheless, he resurfaced in 1995 when he was involved in a financial scheme which led to the Salvation Army losing more than £6 million. Gillick convinced Salvation Army officials that he could offer the charity high returns on its investments. He received a loan of more than £1 million from the charity. The Salvation Army later took legal action to try to force him to repay the loan, plus about £100,000 in interest.

* * *

SCOTTISH SOCCER: A GANGSTERS' PARADISE

Fraudster and security boss Paul Johnston, former owner of Guardion Security, employed some of Glasgow's most feared villains as muscle: Craig Devlin, Paddy Mullen, Stewart 'Specky' Boyd, Michael Bennett and Stephen Scullion. But he also had close links with both Glasgow clubs, Celtic and Rangers. The disgraced former policeman moved to Spain in 2002. At the time, his former police colleagues had a warrant for his arrest but he still kept in regular contact with some players and rogue elements in the supporters' clubs. Guardion Security folded in 2004, owing thousands in unpaid taxes. An underworld source said, 'Johnston has huge amounts of cash. He lives in Spain but his number-one love is football.'

Johnston left the police after being convicted of insurance fraud. He then embarked on a career in the security business with his wife, Marie Healy, whose brother is a convicted drug-smuggler. When Johnston fled to Spain, he was facing fraud and extortion charges relating to Guardion Security. Charges were dropped after he agreed to return, but he has, as yet, failed to come back. In 2004, the government launched an action to ban him and Marie from being company directors after a series of scams. The couple sold off assets including a £1-million mansion in Stewarton, Aryshire, and two taxi firms, presumably fearing they would be targeted under proceeds-of-crime law. They now enjoy the high life on Spain's Costa del Sol. Johnston's right-hand man, former Guardion enforcer and drug-dealer Stewart Boyd, died in a car smash near Johnston's Spanish hideaway in July 2003. Johnston had always wished that he could invest money in a club, but the controversy sparked after another gangster invested in Celtic put him off. Heroin-baron James Hamill, worth £3 million, had thousands of shares in Celtic FC.

15

Global Football Graft

Fortunately, Britain has a long way to go before the influence of criminality reaches the levels of other countries. In eastern Europe, South America and Asia, gangsterism in football is out of control. Although the problem is growing in the UK, the underworld influence is still largely unseen and unofficial. Publicity-shy mobsters in this country still generally prefer to take a back-seat role away from the limelight. They do not, as a rule, sit on the boards of clubs and do not advertise their presence. However, in other countries, gangsters often take over clubs wholesale or use their extraordinary power to routinely corrupt sporting organisations and league tables.

Russian, eastern European and Italian mafias have carved up the game abroad to the extent that mobsters openly flaunt their stakeholdings. In Colombia, rival cocaine cartels own clubs. In other South American countries, football-hooligan crews have brought teams to their knees. Even one of the world's greatest players, Maradona, was 'got to' and lured into the twilight world of drug abuse. The new-found super-wealth of football clubs and their stars has made them magnets for criminals all over the world. In Asia, Chinese mafias led by the Triads routinely fix matches – and their reach even extends to the UK. Remember the floodlight betting scandal of a few years back? Asian betting rings, notoriously highlighted in the Bruce Grobbelaar trials, have had a massive effect on leagues in Britain, Germany, Spain, Italy and the Czech Republic.

In Bulgaria, gangster Georgi Iliev ruled football with an iron fist – until, that is, he was shot dead by a sniper's bullet as he celebrated the victory of Bulgaria's Lokomotiv Plovdiv football club, of which he was the proud proprietor, in a UEFA Cup qualifying round. His last words to the barman were 'More champagne!' at the post-match booze-up.

His chest was ripped apart by the single shot – one of more than sixty expertly executed killings in the former communist state linked to spies. A former wrestling champion, he had served time in jail for theft and gang rape, and ruled his gangland empire with unprecedented brutality, ordering numerous murders and kidnappings and often administering punishment beatings personally. He intimidated rival club bosses and used the game's business to wash his money. Iliev was typical of the new gangster turned football tycoon, leading his men in fights and shoot-outs with rival club officials and supporters, often turning Sofia's nightclubs into battlegrounds. He used his football power to bully himself into politics and infiltrate mainstream business, prompting concern that foreign investors would be frightened away from Bulgaria as a whole. It is widely suspected that the Bulgarian KGB-trained secret service were involved in Iliev's murder. The KGB, before their dissolution in 1991, were experts in their field – in 1978, they infamously killed the Bulgarian dissident Georgi Markov with a ricin-tipped umbrella in London, and in 1981 they were implicated in the attempted murder of Pope John Paul II.

The orders on Iliev were allegedly given after government officials became worried that international football TV coverage was sending a message around the world that it was OK to be a gangster in Bulgaria. Iliev was attracting a lot of attention. Slavco Bosilkov, the former secretary-general of Bulgaria's interior ministry, said, 'There is an ongoing liquidation of the leading figures of the criminal world. It is no coincidence that we have had 60 professional hits in the past four years, but no trial or even a slightest trace of evidence about who would be behind them.'

Bulgarian gangsters often use high-profile violence to protect their drugs, weapons, vice and extortion empires. But an official in a Bulgarian supporters' association said, 'If Iliev had stayed out of football, he would still have been alive. His team was being shown all around the world. Football has become too high profile. He was an embarrassment to the government.'

But Iliev was a pussycat compared with another southern European gangster who had the same idea: Balkan warlord turned football president Arkan. The former Red Star Belgrade hooligan followed his team all around Europe as a teenager, robbing banks and jewellery shops on the way. When the Yugoslavian war kicked off, he formed the notorious Arkan Tigers militia, which raped, killed and looted its way around the battlefields of Bosnia. After returning to his homeland as a national hero, he established himself as Serbia's top gangster and took over Champions League qualifiers Obilic to boost his prestige. He made them in his own image: tough, uncompromising and bullying. And he took them to the top of the league.

Arkan is now dead – killed in a hail of bullets in a Belgrade hotel. But the club, built on the profits of smuggling and the ill-gotten gains of ethnic cleansing, continues. His widow, Ceca, the gangster's glamorous and famous belle, even brought the team to Britain, in the hope of selling players. At a pre-season friendly match in Hull, she declared she wanted to sell Arkan's assets for millions in Britain. 'I'd like to get in touch with the Premier League,' she said. 'We've sold to Holland, France and Russia, but not England.' She enjoys watching English football. 'It's fast and direct,' she explained, praising David Beckham and Ryan Giggs, then of Manchester United, and Michael Owen, then of Liverpool. 'And they're so gentlemanly.' Unlike Arkan, who was wanted by the international criminal tribunal for the former Yugoslavia. His business empire would continue, despite criticism, and it was her job to run Obilic as he would have wished, she said. 'My husband was a builder; he liked to create. He built Obilic from scratch and loved it.'

South America is like a footballing factory exporting top-class players all over the world. Gangsters have been fast to take advantage of the trade, which is said to be more lucrative than selling gold and diamonds. In 2005, Colombian drug-barons attempted to exploit John Viafara's move to Portsmouth. Members of an organised-crime syndicate threatened to kill the president of the club from which Portsmouth bought the international midfielder.

Jose Manuel Lopez, boss of Once Caldas FC, was accused of misleading the mob over the amount Pompey had paid as a transfer fee for the Colombia international. Lopez was put under armed guard following unsubstantiated claims that he had lied over the size of the fee that took Viafara to Fratton Park. The Premiership club had agreed to pay 1.5 million euros (£900,000) for the Colombian, but rumours swept websites that they had paid as much as £1.5 million. Lopez was left in fear of his life when the drug-dealers attempted to extract money after the false rumour reached them. At one point, Lopez was under 24-hour guard.

A frantic call was made to Pompey chief executive Peter Storrie requesting that he make a public declaration about the deal. Storrie said, 'At the request of the Once Caldas president, we were asked to clarify the price we paid for John Viafara. It appeared to us to be a strange request, but we were happy to go along with it. Our understanding is that, having agreed a fee, the fee became hugely exaggerated on websites around the world. From our point, we've done nothing wrong in the deal, and all the relevant paperwork is lodged with the Premier League and the FA.'

While there is no suggestion that Portsmouth did anything wrong, transfers between South American and European clubs have often been hampered by problems. That is why the FA insists that funds from international transfers are paid through a central source and not directly from club to club. Players in South America are often not owned by their clubs but by individuals or companies who frequently have links with the underworld. Several Colombian footballers have been murdered in recent times. Invariably, these have been tied to match-fixing allegations. The most famous concerned Andrés Escobar after the World Cup finals in 1994. Escobar conceded an own goal against the United States, and Colombia were eliminated. Ten days later, the player was shot twelve times as he left a nightclub. With each bullet, his assailant was reported by Escobar's girlfriend to have shouted, 'Goal!'

Illegal betting rings in Malaysia, Indonesia, Singapore and, more recently, China regularly fix games in Europe, South America and Africa. In a major scandal, Brazilian referee Edilson Pereira de Carvalho was banned for life after admitting match-fixing. It culminated in the results of 11 league matches he had refereed being cancelled. Famously, Genoa were demoted from the Serie A to the third division (Serie C) for match-fixing, while Belgium, Portugal, the Czech Republic and Germany were all rocked by corruption or match-fixing probes.

In the highest-profile case, Berlin referee Robert Hoyzer admitted to manipulating four games in the Bundesliga for cash from a Croatian betting syndicate. Mafias in Vietnam and China are even worse. In its maiden season in 2004, China's Super League was left reeling from loud accusations over gambling as well as crooked referees, players and officials on an almost weekly basis. It got so bad that China's cabinet stepped in and ordered a crackdown on match-fixing and hooliganism. In Vietnam, football has come under intense scrutiny, with police investigating fraud allegations implicating some 90 players, referees and coaches in the V-League. The saga took on greater dimensions after several members of the national Under-23 squad were suspected of having fixed games at the request of betting syndicates during the South-East Asian Games. 'We are working on it. We are aware of the situation but it is not easy,' said FIFA president Sepp Blatter. 'It can only be done if everyone is helping us.'

The reach of Asian betting rings only truly came to light in the late '90s, when the floodlights at several British grounds mysteriously failed. They had been sabotaged by gangsters so that games were abandoned when the results were in the Asian bookies' favour. The most sensational plot was hatched at Charlton Athletic's ground three days before a Liverpool game. The plan was concocted in Malaysia and executed by gang members with the collusion of a corrupt Charlton security official. If it had succeeded, it would have netted an estimated £30 million for the criminals that operate Asia's illegal betting industry. British police officers – acting on a tip-off – were lying in wait when Wai Yuen Liu and two Malaysian co-saboteurs arrived at the Valley. Four men in total were arrested, and a search of Liu's car and the Malaysian pair's hotel room revealed enough equipment to wreck the lights at another eight games.

In a period of 15 months, the betting syndicate had already interfered with two Premiership games without arousing the suspicion of British football authorities. The Valley was third on the list. They were significantly helped by a corrupt insider – Charlton security supervisor Roger Firth – who was paid £20,000 for letting the saboteurs into the ground. The police also discovered the names of another two key individuals in the Charlton conspirators' personal belongings. One was employed at West Ham's Upton Park and the other at Wimbledon's home, Selhurst Park, at the times of a blackout occurring at each of those grounds in 1997. Both men were arrested but escaped charges due to lack of evidence.

It was Firth, however, who initiated his own downfall after a clumsy attempt to bribe a fellow security guard with £5,000 to allow the sabotage to go ahead. But the arresting officers from the Metropolitan Police Organised Crime Group only understood the full significance of the case when it was discovered that the tampering at the Valley would have led to complete failure of the lights. When put beside the failures at West Ham and Wimbledon, the attempt to blow the floodlights formed part of a clear pattern.

Firth, 49, and the Malaysians, Eng Hwa Lim, 35, and Chee Kew Ong, 49, later admitted conspiracy to cause a public nuisance. Liu, 38, denied any involvement but was found guilty. The betting system worked principally around encounters between the largest and smallest clubs in the Premier League. For example, in the Liverpool v. Charlton game, the south London side would be given a one- or two-goal handicap. If things went according to plan, the fans would still back Liverpool to win. Assuming that Charlton were still 'ahead' on handicap by the start of the second half, the syndicate would then kill the lights. Under betting rules, the result – and bets made on it – stood if the match was abandoned after half-time, allowing the gangs to rake in huge sums on 'rigged' matches.

In countries where armed gangs still rule the roost, they have used football to vent their violence. Sometimes, this affects England. For instance, when the squad visited Albania and Macedonia it was not lost on local warlords that David Beckham and Michael Owen were attractive kidnap targets. Gun-toting gangsters control large parts of Macedonia, and most people in the country carry firearms. Only weeks before an England game in 2003, three bombs exploded in the capital, Skopje. Five people (including one American citizen) were killed in Skopje in another incident as the result of automatic weapons and a hand grenade. The attacks were politically motivated and not connected to the football, but the shockwaves were felt several hundred miles away at the easily shaken FA's headquarters. To make matters worse, the FC Skopje hooligan groups are connected to the ultra-nationalist ethnic Macedonian political party, where anti-Western feeling is strongest.

Back in the 1980s, Diego Maradona catapulted Napoli football club into the limelight and on to win numerous league and championship titles. The team became a beacon of success amidst the grinding poverty of southern Italy. But he soon found himself targeted by the local mafia, known as the Camorra. Unlike in England, the godfathers didn't make an enemy of him. It was even worse – they became his friend.

In the bars and clubs of downtown Naples, Maradona held court with the capos, a guest of honour. The gangs embraced the Argentinian as one of their own, but soon their motive became clear. They got him addicted to cocaine and bled him dry. When it all went belly up, they spat him out with bitterness and left him broken, not even able to pay his taxes. The football superstar had been destroyed by criminals for a quick profit. The dream finally ended when Napoli Calcio were declared bankrupt, with debts of over€70 million. Many pointed the finger at Mafia entanglements. After losing a bitter legal battle to avoid relegation, Napoli now find themselves flailing in the country's third division, Serie C. And Maradona is turkeying in Cuba, recovering in rehab after a personal plea by Fidel Castro.

Epilogue

Hooligans, Money-Launderers and Agents

Football and Gangsters has covered some of the clear and present dangers facing football today. Taxing, extortion, blackmail and bribery are the main threats to football clubs from the underworld. And, for the moment, there seems little that clubs can do to protect themselves, mainly because the structure of their businesses are intrinsically vulnerable to such attacks. How many high-profile global organisations with £100-million-plus turnovers, hundreds of staff and tens of thousands of customers worldwide have so much of their value tied up in a tiny amount of human capital concentrated in one place – that is, the team on the pitch? Usually, corporations of a similar size have their worth spread out amongst thousands of assets and individuals countrywide, if not worldwide. If one individual is compromised, or one asset lost, the business can in general cope and carry on regardless. In football, a villain only has to get control of one or two key players and they've got a very powerful tool they can use to influence what goes on.

A leading security analyst at a top investment bank has likened football clubs in the UK to gold-bullion reserves in a bank. He said, 'Manchester United and Chelsea are like scaled-down versions of the US Federal

Reserve – having all the gold stored in one place. The difference is the gold at Fort Knox is under armed guard. How many clubs take adequate steps to protect their teams like you would any other asset? Clubs need to take risks like kidnapping seriously. One day, it will happen.'

However, just as clubs are waking up to the evils that lurk beyond the stadium gate, the gangsters of the future may be even worse. For instance, a new phenomenon has brought with it a new terrifying threat – that posed by former football-hooligan gangs who have moved wholesale into organised crime, drug-dealing, security consultancy and protection rackets. Cardiff's Soul Crew, West Ham's Inter City Firm, Arsenal's Gooners and Everton's Snorty Forty are just a few of the gangs containing razor-sharp hoodlums who have grown up to form powerful criminal elites – all based around going to the match. Some of West Ham's top boys now control moody door firms, smuggling cartels and ticket-touting firms. The loosely connected network of fiercely loyal villains make millions from counterfeiting, armed robbery, contract killing, duty fraud and vice, all run within a claret-and-blue empire stretching from Canning Town to Essex and as far as Marbella and Thailand. Soccer hooligans from Millwall, Chelsea, Man United, Man City, Leeds, Newcastle, Celtic and Rangers have all graduated into big-time mobsters of one form or another. How long will it be before they will want to turn on the goose that laid the golden egg? How long before they target the clubs themselves? And who will stop them? How do you stop them? In many cases, they've got the brains, the muscle and, more importantly, the money to get busy in the boardroom of any club they choose.

I have already seen one example with my own eyes in Leeds, where former members of the city's crazed Service Crew claimed to me that they had gained influence over former club directors. In return for patronage, the director asked their top boys to 'keep him sweet with the fans'. That meant keeping the majority of fans in line, making sure that they backed whichever regime was in power and didn't make too much of a fuss when bad decisions were made. In the end, the top boys were so confident of their ability to power-broke, they formed a legal consortium in a bid to buy the club outright.

In other cities, the intrusion has been more subtle. Remember how Cardiff City boss Sam Hammam courted controversy when he employed vicious convicted hooligans turned bodyguards to run his personal and stadium security? Remember how he lapped up the Soul Crew's devotion? He was later criticised for allowing the top boys to have an influence in the official side of things.

Ironically, the reason why gangsters got involved with football in the first place many years ago in the '50s and '60s has now come full circle and is once again one of the greatest threats now and in the future. Money-laundering is especially important to crime organisations today because of the huge sums involved, tighter regulation and the international nature of modern business. Money-laundering is no longer an ad hoc afterthought following a good touch or a big blag. It's no longer just about inflating gate receipts here and there or inventing a phantom revenue stream for a few months to cover a long-firm (whereby criminals buy a company, use it to get lots of credit and stock and then walk away) or a new fraud. Washing money is key to a modern crime empire and is carried out clinically, professionally and sustainably.

In the old days, villains used to get corrupt officials within a legit club to clean their money by falsely inflating gate receipts. Drug-barons today like to buy football clubs outright so they can wash money en masse, systematically, week in, week out. When a proprietor tells the taxman that 20,000 fans attended the last game, how can the taxman prove that it was 10,000? It's very difficult. Football grounds also provide drug-dealers with unique property-development opportunities – an extra bonus for a professional financial fraudster.

Britain's richest-ever criminal and Interpol's Target One Curtis Warren poisoned the hallowed turf by buying a lower-division club in order to launder his illicit narcotics profits. As he flew over the club in a helicopter, he pointed to the ground and gleefully announced that he owned it. His former associate took over another football club, which he continues to run today, despite being investigated by the police for other crimes. A well-known crime family who made their fortune from armed robbery and heroin-dealing also own a football club.

And, last but not least, there are the football professionals whom everyone loves to hate: agents. Despite FIFA player representatives being licensed and regulated, their detractors feel that agents represent a double risk in the game. Some of them are believed, rightly or wrongly, to be corrupt, making them willing collaborators with the underworld, or at least open to coercion. Agency businesses, some of them worth millions of pounds, also offer opportunities for villains to get a legit, easy entry into the game via the back door. The names of FIFA-licensed agents may be listed over the door, but some would claim that in certain cases the real owners, as in Las Vegas, may be mobs. There are several in business in the UK owned secretly by gangsters. In 2004, an interesting article in the *Daily Mail* by veteran sports editor Des Kelly highlighted the murky world of agents under the headline 'AGENTS FIGHT BACK AS FOOTBALL'S DIRTY WAR STARTS TO GET EVEN MORE GRUBBY':

> THEY have been cast as football's underworld, sleazy operators in an extortion racket that drains millions of pounds out of the game every year. Meet the agents.
>
> Using offshore accounts, holding companies and unrecorded cash transactions as their weapons of deception, these dealers are said to be ruthless traffickers, accused of destroying the sport from within.
>
> A growing cross-section of the Premiership hierarchy want to cast them out.

The article revealed how chairmen despise agents, agents dislike clubs and clubs pay for the whole gravy train without really knowing what they are buying. One passage exposed the internal warfare that was going on:

Crystal Palace chairman Simon Jordan described them as 'nasty scum, evil, divisive and pointless'.

Middlesbrough chairman Steve Gibson joined the fray, proclaiming agents were 'liars', 'greedy people' and 'the most unsavoury part of football'.

One warned, 'If clubs want to do the dirty on us, then great, we'll do the same to them. There's plenty of information that could come out and, when it does, we'll see who the real villains are.'

And this war of words is between the top people out in the open. What goes on amongst the shadier ones, behind the scenes in the underworld?

The threat posed by unscrupulous agents should not be underestimated.

At the end of the day, there is only one group of people who can stop the growing pairing of football and gangsters – and that's the fans. Football clubs, the sport's regulatory bodies and the gangsters trying to muscle in all tend not to take sufficient account of the fans. They may pay the wages, but to the people in charge, and to the villains who are desperate to seize power off the owners and managers, they are often viewed as a toothless group of people who are there to be exploited and will continue to support their teams week after week, no matter how badly they are treated.

Sometimes, they are seen as a hassle. Other times, their wishes are ignored completely. However, if the fans decide that organised crime has no place in their game and begin to fight back, they would certainly be a force to be reckoned with – possibly the only real challenge that could or would enable a thorough clean-up of football. In recent years, there have been some encouraging signs that fans can impose their will to great effect, with grass-roots supporters clubs taking on corporate interests in the game and winning. For example, consider the dissenting group of Man United fans who took a stand against the Glazer takeover and set up a new club, attracting 4,000-plus fans at some games. Or the brave stance of Wrexham supporters against a property developer who wanted to take their ground off them. In these cases, the targets of the fans' protests were not gangsters, but the principle of the action is the important lesson: people-power works.

Of course, gangsters are completely different animals from businessmen, but if there's one thing they hate, it's organised resistance and bad publicity. Criminals cannot survive without the tacit consent of the communities they live in. If fans turned their attention to defeating the crooks who want to steal their game from them lock, stock and two smoking barrels, then there is a good chance the villains would be scared off and defeated once and for all.

POWDER WARS

The Supergrass Who Brought Down Britain's Biggest Drug Dealers

GRAHAM JOHNSON

ISBN 9781840189254
Available now
£7.99 (paperback)

Gangster Paul Grimes was a one-man crimewave with a breathtaking capacity to steal. Any villains who got in his way were made to pay – often with their blood. But when his son died of a drugs overdose, the old-school mobster swore revenge on the new generation of Liverpool-based heroin and cocaine dealers. Against all odds, he turned undercover informant.

Two major gangsters fell foul of Grimes's change of heart: Curtis Warren, aka 'Cocky', the wealthiest and most successful criminal in British history, and heroin baron John Haase. But, as his net began to tighten, Grimes was confronted with the ultimate dilemma. He discovered his second son was now a rising star in the drugs business. The life-or-death question was: should he shop him or not?

Today, Paul Grimes has a £100,000 contract on his head and is a real-life dead man walking. *Powder Wars* is a riveting account of modern gangsters told in brutal detail.

'The best gangster book of modern times'

Donal MacIntyre

DRUGLORD

Guns, Powder and Pay-offs

GRAHAM JOHNSON

ISBN 9781845962401
Available now
£7.99 (paperback)

When ruthless drug baron John Haase was sentenced to 18 years' imprisonment for heroin-trafficking in 1995, it was a major victory for Customs and the police. But in a shock move, after Haase and his partner Paul Bennett had served only 11 months, then Home Secretary Michael Howard signed a Royal Pardon for their release.

Howard defended his extraordinary decision by revealing that Haase and Bennett had become invaluable informants. But Haase had in fact duped the authorities and he returned to his life of crime immediately upon his release. Far from being forced into hiding as a supergrass, he had gained new kudos among the criminal underworld for beating the system so audaciously.

Graham Johnson interviewed Haase at Whitemoor prison and has obtained a copy of his sworn affidavit revealing the truth behind the Royal Pardon scandal. Interwoven with secretly taped testimonies from many of Haase's closest associates and co-conspirators, this is an explosive exposé of Britain's number-one drug kingpin.

> 'A serious exposé of modern organised crime that puts the myth of the cheeky, chirpy Liverpool scally firmly into perspective . . . a cracking read'
>
> *Tribune*

THE HAPPY DUST GANG

How Sex, Scandal and Deceit Founded a Drugs Empire

DAVID LESLIE

ISBN 9781845962616
Available now
£7.99 (paperback)

Charlie, snow, toot, white: cocaine goes by many different names. In Glasgow in the early 1980s, they called it happy dust.

At no-holds-barred parties of the glamorous and wealthy, cocaine fuelled the loss of inhibitions and the realisation of fantasies. It was the new aphrodisiac, for which beautiful models would shed their clothes and ordinary housewives would forget their vows. A few lines of Charlie and a humdrum party could become an orgy.

The trail led from the forests of Colombia to Glasgow streets where butchers and bakers, fruiterers and Ferrari drivers passed Charlie along the line to the cocktail set, yuppies desperate for kicks and thrills, young people in clubs and discotheques, and highly paid sports stars. Behind it all was a man they called the Parachutist.

But all too soon, the party was over. People became too greedy, and the Parachutist was double-crossed. Some of the gang did shady deals with detectives in hotel rooms; others flew to seek shelter in the sun, their reputations destroyed but not their fortunes. For the Happy Dust Gang, the good times might have been over, but their legacy lives on to this day.

CRIMELORD: THE LICENSEE

The True Story of Tam McGraw
DAVID LESLIE

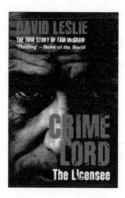

ISBN 9781845961664
Available now
£7.99 (paperback)

Crimelord is the gripping life story of elusive multi-millionaire gangster Tam McGraw. A notorious criminal kingpin, McGraw has risen from extreme poverty in the East End of Glasgow to become one of Scotland's wealthiest men.

When hash started to flood into Scotland from the late 1980s onwards, suspicion centred on McGraw, leader of the infamous Barlanark Team. After a two-year surveillance operation, police discovered the drug had been hidden in buses carrying young footballers and deprived Glasgow families on free holidays abroad. Police claimed McGraw was the financier and mastermind, but in 1998 a jury declared him innocent while other suspects were jailed.

As McGraw refuses to discuss his life publicly, his remarkable tale is told through friends, fellow crooks and the occasional rival. It is an outrageous, often hilarious, true gangster story.

> 'Thrilling'
> *News of the World*

> 'An outrageous, often hilarious, but always fascinating account of the Glasgow underworld'
> *Irvine Times*